D0230572

Management

Managing in a Downturn

FT Prentice Hall
FINANCIAL TIMES

In an increasingly competitive world, we believe it's quality of thinking that gives you the edge – an idea that opens new doors, a technique that solves a problem, or an insight that simply makes sense of it all. The more you know, the smarter and faster you can go.

That's why we work with the best minds in business and finance to bring cutting-edge thinking and best learning practice to a global market.

Under a range of leading imprints, including *Financial Times Prentice Hall*, we create world-class print publications and electronic products bringing our readers knowledge, skills and understanding, which can be applied whether studying or at work.

To find out more about Pearson Education publications, or tell us about the books you'd like to find, you can visit us at **www.pearsoned.co.uk**

PEARSON

FINANCIAL TIMES
MASTERING MANAGEMENT

Managing in a Downturn

Leading business thinkers on how to grow when markets don't

WITHDRAWN

SAID BUSINESS SCHOOL
EXECUTIVE EDUCATION LIBRARY

**Financial Times
Prentice Hall
is an imprint of**

Harlow, England • London • New York • Boston • San Francisco • Toronto • Sydney • Singapore • Hong Kong
Tokyo • Seoul • Taipei • New Delhi • Cape Town • Madrid • Mexico City • Amsterdam • Munich • Paris • Milan

PEARSON EDUCATION LIMITED

Edinburgh Gate
Harlow CM20 2JE
Tel: +44 (0)1279 623623
Fax: +44 (0)1279 431059
Website: www.pearsoned.co.uk

First published in Great Britain in 2009
© Financial Times 2009
ISBN: 978-0-273-73005-7

British Library Cataloguing-in-Publication Data
A catalogue record for this book is available from the British Library

Library of Congress Cataloging-in-Publication Data
Managing in a downturn : leading business thinkers on how to grow when markets don't.
          p. cm.
    Includes bibliographical references and index.
    ISBN 978-0-273-73005-7 (pbk. : alk. paper) 1. Management. 2. Business cycles. 3.
Business planning. 4. Recessions.
    HD31.M294145 2009
    658--dc22

                                        2009020861

All rights reserved. No part of this publication may be reproduced, stored in a retrieval
system, or transmitted in any form or by any means, electronic, mechanical, photocopying,
recording, or otherwise without either the prior written permission of the publishers or a
licence permitting restricted copying in the United Kingdom issued by the Copyright
Licensing Agency Ltd, Saffron House, 6–10 Kirby Street, London EC1N 8TS. This book may
not be lent, resold, hired out or otherwise disposed of by way of trade in any form of binding
or cover other than that in which it is published, without the prior consent of the Publishers.

10 9 8 7 6 5 4 3 2 1
13 12 11 10 09

Typeset by Stone Serif 9pt/13pt by 30
Printed by Ashford Colour Press Ltd., Gosport
The publisher's policy is to use paper manufactured from sustainable forests.

Contents

Foreword

In the current economic and financial climate, it is difficult for many businesspeople to think beyond the doom and gloom dominating the headlines. Since the credit crunch began in earnest in August 2007, when the European Central Bank injected €95bn worth of funds into the money markets, it has continued to gather momentum and threaten or destroy some of the biggest names in the business. From Bear Stearns and Lehman Brothers to General Motors and Woolworths, the fall-out from the first severe downturn of the 21st century has yet to play itself out.

For senior managers and executives, navigating through turbulent times is never easy. The instinctive reaction is to cut costs and hunker down until things get better. But retreating into a shell is not always the right decision for the long term. Indeed, a downturn can present a good opportunity for companies to reposition themselves, scour the market for deals, recruit talent from competitors and, ultimately, equip themselves for sustainable long-term success.

Managing in a Downturn was first published in the Financial Times and on FT.com, and brings together the world's leading business thinkers to consider some of the big questions confronting managers. What lessons – if any – can be learnt from previous downturns and how organisations functioned in those difficult times? What can businesses do to minimise the short-term pain and maximise long-term competitive advantage? And what will the future business environment look like?

We do not claim to have all the answers, but hope we can offer some signposts for the difficult journey ahead.

part

one

Surveying the damage

Time for managers to stand and deliver

With many managers facing their first downturn and companies struggling to form a credible crisis plan, new business thinking offers some useful context and guidance. By **Stefan Stern**

It's just like old times. Unemployment is soaring, order books are shrinking. The phones that used to keep ringing have fallen uncharacteristically silent. And the taxi ride across town, which until recently could take anything up to an hour on a bad day, can now be knocked off in under half that time.

Welcome to the global recession 2009. For some managers, this is a new (and unpleasant) experience. They have never known markets like this before. For more than a decade, business, while not necessarily easy, seemed relatively steady and predictable. There was growth, low inflation and rising demand. The graphs kept heading the right way.

Today, the younger dogs are having to learn some new tricks, while the more venerable hounds find their memory banks being raided for experience and advice. What do you do when demand dries up? How can you cut costs without cutting your own throat? In the words of Adrian Slywotzky at management consultancy Oliver Wyman: how do you grow when markets don't?

This new series of Mastering Management could not be better timed. In delayered and streamlined businesses a good deal of corporate memory has been lost. Who in today's C-suite had serious managerial responsibility at the time of the global recession in the early 1980s? Even the downturn of the early 1990s feels like ancient history to a lot of today's senior executives.

This is where the contributors to this new series can help. Academic writing on business has been criticised for being too narrowly focused and impractical. Managers have been happy to study and collect their MBAs but then leave their business school tutors far behind. At the same time, academics have had to defend themselves against the charge of irrelevance.

But in a naughty world, universities, at their best, pursue objective knowledge about timeless (and recurring) human challenges. They are not biddable. Academics will tell you straight what they know and what they have found. Not all management consultants can make the same claim.

❝In delayered and streamlined businesses a good deal of corporate memory has been lost❞

The editors of this series have commissioned a range of leading business school experts and commentators to offer their observations on the difficulties of managing in the current downturn. No serious management discipline or dilemma escapes their scrutiny.

First, we look at the context of the current downturn and what lessons can be drawn from previous recessions, including the Scandinavian, and Japanese crises in the 1990s, and what management remedies (if any) can be applied today. We also encourage readers to lift their eyes from the current gloom and consider how business leaders can seize this moment to position themselves for the upturn.

Looking to leaders

In the following three issues, authors will consider other major issues facing corporate leadership teams: the question of managing people effectively in a downturn; what to do about supply chains that are coming under pressure and how to reconfigure them to your advantage; how to market to customers who themselves face hard times; how to approach possible mergers and acquisitions activity; the role of the board during a downturn; and the essentials of communicating with internal and external stakeholders successfully.

Management teams need help. Just how much they need it became clear with the release of a new global survey conducted earlier this year by the consultants Booz & Co. As many as 40 per cent of the senior managers surveyed said they doubted their leadership had a credible plan to deal with the current crisis. A slightly larger number, 46 per cent, doubt the leadership team is capable of carrying out its plans, whether they are credible or not.

Before you move on to the business thinkers' take on all this, however, here is one management writer's perspective on the downturn and how to deal with it.

There are only so many ways you can tell a company to 'conserve cash'. It will probably turn out to be the business catchphrase of 2009. But while managers are understandably in a hurry to stem the flow of cash out of the building, in particular by reducing headcount, they risk cutting too deeply into the flesh of the organisation, and making future recovery much harder to achieve. Easy advice for an outsider to give – and hard for a manager to take when survival is the number one priority – but sound advice all the same. Don't get rid of the people who actually make your products and services worth buying in the first place.

Second, the rumour mill is almost as big an enemy to senior management right now as collapsing customer demand. All the management gurus agree that leaders have to invest much more time than they might think is necessary into communicating with their staff. And 'communicating' means listening as well as telling. In his most recent book *The Leadership Code*, Dave Ulrich estimates that a message may have to be communicated as many as 10 times, in a variety of means or channels, for it to get through and be understood.

" Academics will tell you straight what they know. Not all management consultants can make the same claim "

Offering as much certainty as possible will also help kill rumours. Binna Kandola, managing partner of business psychologists Pearn Kandola, argues that knowing you have lost your job is a better outcome for most employees than being in the dark about your future.

Third, keeping your head down, retreating from markets and turning introspective, while a natural human response to bad news, is a terrible option for businesses. Now is not the time to abandon partnerships and joint ventures, or to close yourself off to other outside influences. Keep an open mind to new initiatives, remain an active networker and ensure the organisation is not collectively burying its head in the sand.

Fourth, remember that recovery will come – eventually. Research and development needs to continue. Revenue streams that may have temporarily dried up will start to flow again. But capacity that you cut back on now may be hard to resurrect. And again, excessive redundancies – which carry a significant cost in any case – will deprive you of the talent you need to make the most of the upturn. You will only have to hire it back again, at great expense, in a year's time.

Nobody said that being a senior manager would be easy. That's partly why it's called 'compensation', and not pay. But in truth, a lot of managers have had it relatively easy for the past 10 years. Now it is time to stand and deliver.

2

Keeping the global economy afloat

History shows that prompt and aggressive policy decisions and bold restructuring are the only ways to avoid a lengthy malaise. By **Ilian Mihov**

To understand the dynamics of the global crisis, it is useful to start with a historical perspective. Over the past 130 years, US income per capita (adjusted for inflation) has increased by an average of 1.85 per cent a year (see Figure 2.1 below). The solid line shows that from $3,300 in 1870, US per capita income has increased to more than $45,000 in 2007.

There are three important lessons from this. First, most of the time the increase in income proceeds in a smooth pattern; recessions are short and barely noticeable; expansions are smooth and relatively long. Second, there is one calamity that stands out in this graph – the Great Depression of 1929-33. There is nothing in US economic history that even vaguely resembles this trauma. Third, the graph shows that no matter what happens – mild recessions, depressions, rapid expansions (such as the second world war) – the US economy has always returned to the trend of 1.85 per cent growth in per capita income (the straight line).

The facts about the Great Depression are staggering. From growth rates of between 3 and 10 per cent in per capita terms, the US economy imploded: contracting 11 per cent in 1930, another 9.5 per cent the following year, and then shrinking a further 15 per cent in 1932. After surging during the 1920s, share prices on Wall Street plummeted, with the Dow Jones Industrial Average falling to a low of 41.22 points in 1932 from 381.17 points in September 1929.

To put that in context today, it would be equivalent to the Dow falling to 1,666 points from a peak of 14,164 (October 9 2007) within just two years. While the stock market fell some 90 per cent, the output of the US economy fell by one-third during the Great Depression, unemployment shot up to 25.2 per cent from 3.2 per cent, and one-third of the 24,000 banks in the US closed down. This is a partial, yet telling view of the magnitude of the Great Depression. It was so traumatic because the economy became trapped in a vicious circle, in which banks' balance sheets worsened because of a deterioration in economic conditions and the economy declined because banks did not lend since their balance sheets deteriorated.

How does this compare with today's crisis and what can be done to ensure that the global economy does not again fall into such a vicious circle?

Causes of the current crisis

By now there is widespread agreement on the proximate and fundamental causes of the current downturn. The immediate reason for the start of the crisis was the housing market bubble in the US, which began to deflate in 2006. Other factors – such as subprime lending, securitisation, leverage and opacity of financial instruments – magnified the problems resulting from the decline in housing prices. The deeper question is: why did this bubble with all its complications develop? What went wrong in the sophisticated signalling mechanisms that are supposed to warn any policymaker that deep imbalances are in the process of developing?

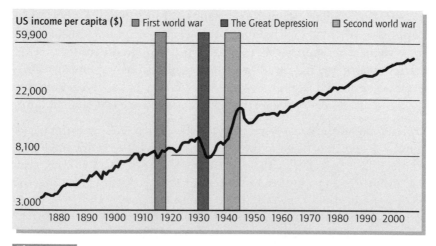

Figure 2.1   Historical perspective of current global crisis

The rapid growth in China at the start of this decade combined with a high savings rate created a continuously increasing pool of liquidity. Some of these savings were used to purchase US Treasury bonds, which pushed yields on US debt to historical lows. The 'savings glut' from China, other emerging economies and oil-producing countries generated low interest rates, which facilitated borrowing.

While in the long end of the yield curve there was a clear movement down, on the short end the US Federal Reserve also pushed the Fed funds rate down to 1 per cent. Today, many observers blame Alan Greenspan, then Fed chairman, for driving down the rate to 1 per cent but he did this because between 2002 and 2004 US inflation was getting dangerously close to the deflationary zone. At the time, policymakers and market participants were predicting that the US would enter a period of deflation and this would be the path to repeating either the Great Depression or at least the Japanese slowdown of the 1990s. Few central bankers would have reacted differently.

Probably the deepest cause for the crisis is the inconsistency in the way the financial sector is regulated. While commercial banks are regulated and supervised quite closely, investment banks and other financial institutions have very light regulation. Commercial banks had the incentive to originate mortgage loans and remove them from their balance sheets by securitising them and selling the new securities to funds, investment banks or other investors. Since mortgages were transferred off the balance sheet of commercial banks, the loan officers had almost no incentives to monitor the quality of borrowers. The fact that some entities are closely regulated but others are not is a big part of the problem.

The picture so far suggests that the massive increase in liquidity generated falling long-term interest rates, low inflation justified low short-term interest rates, and both of these developments led to higher demand for borrowing in developed markets. Banks were lending and reshuffling loans into securitised instruments.

The credit rating agencies also played their part by rating certain portions of these securities with the highest possible rating, implying very low probability of default. In other words, they prepared the market for the mispricing of these securities. Because these securities were complex, few investors could understand the underlying risks and, therefore, they relied on the credit rating agencies. Once the agencies certified them as safe investments, demand for these securities soared. With demand high, US banks had incentives to create more securities without paying too much attention to the risks associated with the borrowers to whom they lent. It was this detachment of the loan originator (a US bank) and the ultimate investor in this highly complicated security that led to the breakdown of the standard monitoring of the quality of borrowers.

The shock resulting from the collapse of the house price bubble was bad enough but what is worse is that it has been amplified by the collapse of the financial sector, which has pushed the economy into a Depression-style vicious circle. In this situation, financial institutions tend to reduce lending, which slows real economic activity and, as a result, the number of defaults on bank loans increases. These defaults feed back to the financial sector by straining banks' balance sheets. Under these conditions, the financial sector further reduces lending and the economy fluctuates between real collapse and financial collapse.

> ❝ Probably the deepest cause for the crisis is the inconsistency in the way the financial sector is regulated ❞

Empirically, we do not know whether market forces will restore equilibrium without intervention. During the Great Depression, policymakers tried to see how deep a recession would go if left to the market. We do not know whether they ever reached bottom because the Depression was brought to an end by government intervention. Every deflationary financial crisis since has ended either with a massive monetary policy injection or fiscal expansion, or both.

What happens next?

Given the similarities between the current crisis and the Great Depression (in terms of shocks and amplification mechanisms), it is useful to keep the historical perspective and look at how the Great Depression ended. Franklin D. Roosevelt was inaugurated as the 32nd US president on March 4 1933. Immediately, he started working on four fronts to stop the deflationary spiral: limit the pervasive banking panic and reconstruct the financial sector; suspend the Gold Standard and allow the Fed to use monetary policy to increase liquidity aggressively; prepare a broad-based fiscal expansion; and change the regulatory environment. The US economy started to recover rapidly, with growth rates of 8 to 10 per cent during the next few years.

The current crisis may be resolved along similar lines. The first set of actions taken in October and November 2008 were designed to stabilise the financial sector. This step is essential because without banks lending, the economy goes down into a vicious downward spiral. The second line of dealing with the crisis involves monetary policy. It is difficult to overemphasise how aggressive and unorthodox US monetary policy has been in the last quarter of 2008.

The Fed started with a rather standard response to the crisis by lowering interest rates in 2007 and 2008. The collapse of Lehman Brothers in September of last year changed the game. The massive injections of capital in the US and in other advanced economies did not generate the necessary revitalisation of the lending process.

In an unprecedented move, on October 27 2008 the Fed opened its lending window to start lending directly to non-financial institutions in the commercial paper market. In a matter of two weeks, the facility – which buys commercial paper – ballooned from zero to more than $250bn. Without this lending, companies would not have received short-term funds to pay suppliers or workers, or would have received funds from commercial banks at a substantially higher cost. One can only speculate where the economy would have ended up without this lending directly from the central bank.

The commercial paper lending facility is only one of several lending facilities opened by the Fed in the past 12 months. The injection of liquidity by the Fed in the past few months has seen its balance sheet explode from $900bn to more than $2,200bn since September.

The third pillar relates to fiscal policy. By cutting taxes or increasing spending, the government can prop up demand in the economy and stop the vicious circle. There is little doubt that a well-designed fiscal package can shorten the recession dramatically and make it much shallower than it would be without a fiscal stimulus. How big should that stimulus be? The package must have three critical components: immediate implementation; an initial instalment of between $500bn and $1,000bn; and an expectations-setting component that states that there will be an additional stimulus package further down the road.

Finally, one can easily anticipate a wave of regulatory changes. Our perceptions about the financial system during the past 70 years were shaped to a large extent by the Great Depression. The process of disintermediation by commercial banks during the Depression was seen as a major amplifying force for the crisis. Regulation (for example, the 1933 Glass-Steagall Act, which prevented commercial banks from engaging in the investment business) focused most of the attention on regulating commercial banks, leaving investment banks much less regulated. With the repeal of the Glass-Steagall Act in 1999 and with the rapid advance of financial innovation, the investment banking sector has become closely intertwined with commercial banks and, therefore, regulators can no longer afford to leave investment banking activities with the degree of supervision that existed previously. The new regulatory framework will have to address the asymmetry between the importance of investment banks in liquidity provision and their status as less regulated entities.

A common misconception

There is a concern that the massive injections of liquidity by the Fed will create inflation and even hyperinflation in the US. This misconception is based on the assumption that the money created by the Fed will translate at some point into purchasing power that will put pressure on prices. Indeed, between September 10 2008 and November 5 2008, the monetary base in the US – the money supply fully controlled by the Fed – increased by almost 50 per cent. Under normal circumstances, this would create too much liquidity in the system that would translate eventually into lending and spending. This increase in spending would push up prices and inflation would soon materialise.

However, in the current environment this is not happening. The liquidity created by the Fed is stored in the vaults of commercial banks and there is almost no increase in broader measures of money. Banks are required to keep a certain amount of deposits as cash in their vaults (or as deposits in the central bank). It is in their interest to keep as little cash as possible because it is by lending money that they earn interest. In normal times, the US banking sector keeps about $2bn in so-called excess reserves – cash above and beyond what is required by law. In the four months following the collapse of Lehman, the excess reserves have ballooned from $2bn to almost $800bn. The commercial banking sector in the US is required by law to keep about $53bn dollars in reserves, but the actual number is $852bn.

> **Whether the adjustment will be smooth or abrupt and painful depends on the actions of policymakers**

If the Fed finds that the money they have injected into the economy starts to create inflationary pressures (that is, lending resumes), then they can slowly or quickly (it is their choice) mop up the excess liquidity. They can do this in several ways: by closing down some of the newly created lending facilities or by a straightforward increase in interest rates. Will it work? It did in Japan. During the country's period of quantitative easing, the monetary base increased rapidly, with the base nearly doubling between 2002 and 2006. As quantitative easing came to an end, the bank promptly withdrew the excess money and thus avoided a rise in inflation.

Conclusion

For almost a decade, many economists warned that the global imbalances that developed in the late 1990s and early 2000s were unsustainable. Excessive consumption in the US and high savings rates in emerging markets created large US trade deficits financed by China and other emerging economies. In some ways, the global financial crisis is the resolution of these global imbalances. Consumption in the US will have to be reduced to more sustainable levels and the disappearance of the wealth effect from the high house prices will facilitate this adjustment.

As the graph of US income per capita shows, the US economy historically has always returned to a steady growth of 1.85 per cent. The big debate is whether we need a long and painful deviation like the Great Depression to get there.

Whether the adjustment will be smooth or abrupt and painful depends on the actions of policymakers. Any projection about a recession or recovery for 2009 or 2010 has to specify explicitly what kind of policy actions are anticipated in this period. With prompt and aggressive monetary and fiscal policy and a well-developed programme to restructure the financial sector, the recession might indeed end in 2009. There is only one way to create a calamity like the Great Depression: by ruining the financial sector and sitting on the sidelines waiting for self-correction mechanisms to kick in.

In 2000, before becoming Fed chairman, Ben Bernanke wrote one of the most informative accounts of the Japanese decline in the 1990s. His prescriptions involved aggressive and non-orthodox policy measures. Today he is implementing his own recommendations through the lending facilities introduced by the Fed. His article ended with: 'Perhaps it's time for some Rooseveltian resolve in Japan.' Today it is time for some Rooseveltian resolve in the US and across the world.

The big freeze

Investigating the credit crisis and liquidity. By **Murillo Campello**, **John Graham** & **Campbell Harvey**

M ost introductory finance courses start by assuming that capital markets are perfect and that companies and banks are able to borrow and lend freely. In this hypothetical setting, corporate executives are free to make decisions that maximise the value of their companies and stock prices.

However, the reality is that capital markets are not perfect. There are significant obstructions that prevent companies from making optimal choices and maximising shareholder value. But just how severe are these imperfections? And how big an obstacle are real-world constraints in terms of limiting opportunities to corporate executives? These are hard questions to answer because, unlike medical scientists, economics researchers are rarely able to conduct controlled experiments that treat some companies while administering placebos to others. Instead, financial economists often study exogenous shocks to the corporate sector, to see how companies with different characteristics are affected, and to get a feel for the magnitudes and effects of real-world capital market imperfections.

As devastating as the current crisis has been to the livelihood of many, it also represents an enormous shock to the corporate sector that can aid economic research. We study this shock to learn about the ability of the sector to adapt to adverse circumstances, and to better understand how the availability of liquidity affects corporate decision making. Liquidity can be thought of as the oil that lubricates the economic machinery.

When liquidity dries up, to what extent does this cause the economic infrastructure to seize up and destroy corporate value?

To better understand how the credit crisis has affected the corporate sector, in a joint effort last November with CFO magazine, we surveyed 1,050 chief financial officers in the US, Europe and Asia about how they were managing the liquidity needs of their companies. The results were striking: we found that financially constrained companies were quickly burning through their cash reserves and were having great difficulty finding new sources of funding. The current lack of liquidity is causing these companies to make drastic cuts to capital spending, hiring, and research and development, thereby threatening their very survival.

Burning cash

We began by benchmarking how much cash companies had on their balance sheets in November 2008 versus how much cash they had in November 2007. In the US, the typical firm had cash and liquid assets equal to about 15 per cent of asset value in 2007. The crisis has not affected cash holdings of unconstrained companies, which remain steady at 15 per cent of asset value in 2008. In stark contrast, the cash reserves at financially constrained companies have fallen one-fifth, from 15 per cent to about 12 per cent of book assets. (We classify a company as being financially constrained if the CFO says it has been affected by the cost or availability of external financing.)

A similar pattern of cash burn for constrained companies is evident in Europe and Asia. In Europe, constrained companies typically hold less cash than in the US, while in Asia they hold more. Yet constrained companies' cash holdings fell about 23 per cent in Europe and 11 per cent in Asia. All of these patterns are depicted in Figure 3.1. This evidence implies that the credit crisis is affecting some companies greatly, while having less of an effect on the most profitable companies in the economy.

The speed with which constrained companies across the world are burning through cash reserves is alarming. This problem could become severe if these companies have limited access to other untapped sources of liquidity. We therefore investigated corporate access to bank lines of credit. It is generally difficult to gather representative data on line of credit (LC) access. Much of the data available is restricted to public US corporations, so this analysis is novel.

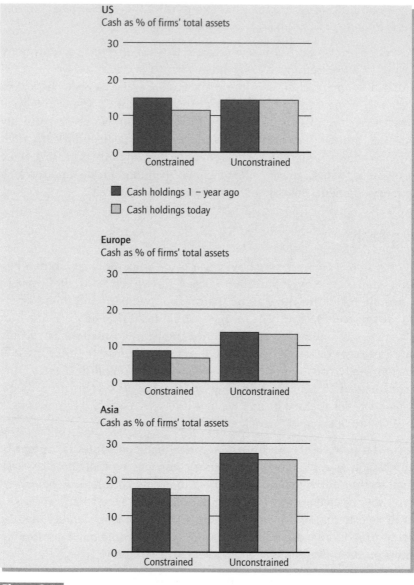

US
Cash as % of firms' total assets

Europe
Cash as % of firms' total assets

Asia
Cash as % of firms' total assets

Figure 3.1

Access to lines of credit

We asked financial executives about the size of the LCs to which they have access and compared LC access now in November 2008 to their lines of credit a year earlier. The typical firm in the US has a pre-arranged line of credit of approximately 19 per cent (unconstrained companies) to 27 per cent (constrained companies) of total book asset value. The differences are more dramatic in Europe and Asia, where constrained companies have committed credit lines of more than 30 per cent of asset value. We find no significant changes in the access to lines of credit in the US (across either constrained or unconstrained companies). In Europe, constrained companies are using 21 per cent more LCs than before while in Asia they are using 10 per cent less. Unconstrained companies in those non-US economies have not changed their use of LCs.

We next asked the companies what they do with the proceeds when they draw down lines of credit. Roughly half of the CFOs said they used the funds for daily operations or short-term liquidity needs. Companies that are financially constrained use their LCs significantly more than do unconstrained counterparts as a way of funding normal business activities.

More surprisingly, 13 per cent of constrained US companies indicated that they had recently drawn on their credit lines in order to have cash for future needs. This purely precautionary use of LCs hints at the following finding: one in six constrained US companies has drawn down on its credit line, in case its banks deny it a line of credit in the future. That is to say there has been a bank run on lines of credit, with many companies drawing on LCs in case they do not have access in the future. Harvard University professors Victoria Ivashina and David Scharfstein have shown that this run on LC borrowing has been large enough to offset the overall tightness of available funding pervading the financial sector. In other words, there has been so much 'just in case' use of bank LCs by financially constrained companies that it appears to have crowded out normal borrowing opportunities, even though the total volume of borrowing remained high throughout 2008. This effect is slightly stronger in Asia, where 18 per cent of surveyed constrained companies reported this behaviour, while in Europe that proportion was 15 per cent. By comparison, only about 6 per cent of unconstrained companies in the US, Asia and Europe said they were drawing on their credit lines for fear that their banks would restrict access to their outstanding lines of credit. These patterns are depicted in Figure 3.2.

> " There has been a bank run on lines of credit with many companies using them to cover future cash needs "

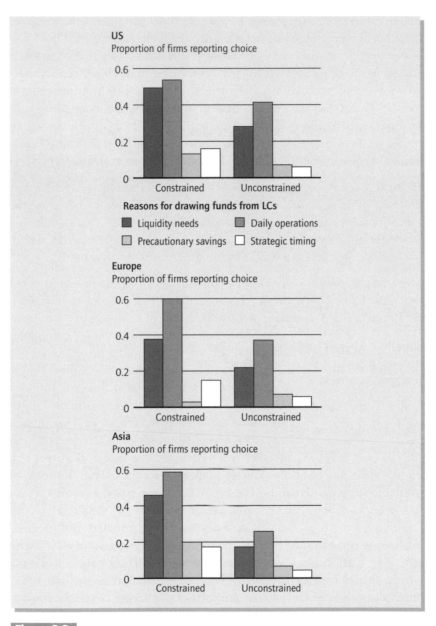

Figure 3.2

As robust as credit drawdowns have been, some companies have resisted using their LCs. We asked why. The most common explanation was that CFOs wanted to preserve borrowing capacity in case it was needed in the future. The second most common explanation for not fully drawing the LC was to maintain a strong reputation in the eyes of financial institutions. This explanation was significantly stronger among public companies and speculative US companies. In Europe, preserving reputation in the eyes of bankers was significantly stronger among financially constrained companies.

Credit problems and investment decisions

So far, we have documented that financially constrained companies across the world have burnt through cash during the past year and have more actively managed lines of credit, including drawing down on them in case their banks limit future access to credit lines. We next examined the degree to which these credit problems have seeped into the real sector, affecting the operating and investment decisions of corporations, with a close eye on the effects on financially constrained companies.

To study this issue, we examined the pro forma plans of companies, conditional on whether they were financially constrained. We found that most companies planned to cut employment, research and development spending, capital investment, marketing expenditures, and (on average) dividends in 2009. The results were significantly worse for financially constrained companies. Constrained companies headquartered in the US planned to dramatically reduce employment (11 per cent), R&D spending (22 per cent), capital investment (9 per cent), marketing expenditures (33 per cent) and dividends (14 per cent) in 2009. Constrained companies in Europe intended to cut employment 8 per cent, R&D spending 5 per cent, capital investment 10 per cent, marketing expenditures 11 per cent, while their dividends were being slashed in half. We see similar patterns in Asia, except that no companies there (constrained and unconstrained) are forecasting cuts in employment.

We also studied the long-term value implications of slashing corporate investment. Most first-year corporate finance courses demonstrate how a company's managers can maximise stockholder value by choosing positive net present value projects. This means that if the returns on an investment out-earn the cost of capital required to fund the project, it creates value for the company. These value-enhancing investments in turn increase shareholder wealth as the stock market capitalises the increased value into the share price. Therefore, if the credit crisis is causing companies to cancel value-enhancing projects, this real world 'constraint' is destroying shareholder value.

To investigate this, we asked companies about the extent to which credit constraints limit their ability to pursue positive net present value investments. We began by benchmarking how often companies say they have to bypass attractive investment projects because of financial constraints. In the US, in normal credit markets, 46 per cent of constrained companies say they pass up attractive investment opportunities due to financial constraints. These are companies that declared themselves to be constrained in late autumn 2008. Undoubtedly, some of these companies would be constrained, and others not, in normal times. One interpretation of our result is therefore that 46 per cent of these companies are constrained during normal times. The 46 per cent of self-declared constrained companies that say they pass up attractive investments is significantly greater than the 20 per cent of unconstrained companies that say the same. In Europe and Asia, more than twice as many constrained companies pass up value-enhancing projects due to credit constraints. In particular, 44 per cent of the constrained European companies in our survey said they bypassed profitable opportunities because of the cost or availability of credit, compared with only 18 per cent of the unconstrained companies. In Asia, the same comparison was 47 per cent for constrained companies versus 20 per cent for unconstrained ones.

Because we conducted our analysis during a severe credit crisis, we are able to investigate the effects of financial constraints on investment during extreme circumstances. A surprising 86 per cent of constrained US companies said they bypassed attractive investments during the credit crisis due to difficulties in raising external finance, about twice as great as the proportion of unconstrained companies that say the same. Again, these numbers are mirrored in Europe and Asia (80 per cent versus 36 per cent in Europe, and 69 per cent versus 29 per cent in Asia).

> Downturns present opportunities that companies should take to restructure, reorganise and invest in plans for the future

We next asked how companies fund attractive investments when they are unable to borrow in financial markets. About half of US companies said they relied on internally generated cash flows to fund investment under these circumstances, and about four in 10 said they used cash reserves. Notably, 56 per cent of constrained US companies said they cancelled investment projects when they were unable to fund them with external funds, significantly greater than the 31 per cent of unconstrained companies that said the same. Once again, we found the same results in Europe and in Asia. In Europe, for example, 69 per cent of the constrained companies in our survey said they would cancel their investment plans (compared with 33 per cent of unconstrained companies). In Asia, that same comparison suggested a cancellation rate of 41 per cent across constrained companies and only 16 per cent across unconstrained ones. To our knowledge, this is the first time that constraint-driven project cancellation has been documented in economic research.

These numbers dramatically illustrate that real-world constraints are a severe deterrent to the ability of companies to pursue value-maximising policies. We also found evidence of another significant disruption to optimal investment that is imposed by severely disrupted credit markets. Not only do companies cancel investment due to tight credit markets, some sell assets to obtain cash. We found that the vast majority of financially constrained companies sold assets in order to fund operations in 2008. Seventy per cent of the constrained respondents in our US survey said they were selling more assets in late 2008 than previously, compared with 37 per cent of the unconstrained respondents, in order to obtain funds. We also found evidence of heavy use of asset sales across constrained companies Europe (61 per cent) and Asia (43 per cent).

Conclusion

The focus of the current credit crisis is on its immediate implications, such as reduced profits and increased unemployment. In contrast, we show that there are worrisome long-term economic consequences of the crisis through its effect on financially constrained companies.

Using a survey of more than 1,000 CFOs in the US, Europe and Asia, we found that organisations were cutting back or cancelling projects that they knew added to company value. The elimination of profitable projects were especially acute for companies that faced financial constraints.

One of the basic tenets of finance is that projects that enhance firm value should be pursued. Financial constraints potentially prevent the funding of these projects. The current credit crisis is an ideal setting to measure the impact of constraints on value creation.

Turning down or cancelling profitable projects is a lesser-known cost of the current financial crisis. In the scramble for short-term cash flow, companies are sacrificing long-term value. This implies lower future growth opportunities and lower future employment growth.

Scandinavia: Failed banks, state control and a rapid recovery

Sweden and Norway made financial crisis a very public affair.
By **B. Espen Eckbo**

The Scandinavian financial crisis of the early 1990s followed a period of financial liberalisation in the 1980s. These policies included liberalisation of bank lending volume, removal of interest rate caps, modernisation of bank capital requirements, and the introduction of relatively high-risk financial products.

This liberalisation caused a rapid expansion in the volume of bank loans made available for speculative investment and banks became much more sensitive to creditor default rates. In this more fragile state, negative economy-wide shocks exposed the illiquidity of the banks' loan portfolios and threatened the solvency of the banking system.

After a big drop in the world oil price in 1986, Norway (a significant oil-exporting country) experienced a shift in its current account from a surplus to a deficit, which in turn triggered a devaluation of the Norwegian krone in 1986 (Norway was pursuing a fixed exchange rate policy at the time). A recession began in 1988, which started a financial crisis among the country's savings banks, followed by the collapse of major commercial banks and the real estate market in 1990–92.

Sweden also experienced a recession and the country's largest savings bank collapsed in 1991, followed by a collapse of two of its largest commercial banks. Property prices had dropped and the country experienced a currency crisis in the autumn of 1992. The crisis ended in 1993 in both countries.

According to calculations by the International Monetary Fund, the cumulative fall in real gross domestic product over the crisis period was greater for Sweden than for its neighbour (5.3 per cent versus 0.1 per cent). Loan losses in the peak crisis year amounted to 2.8 per cent of GDP in Norway and 3.8 per cent in Sweden, while non-performing loans added up to 9 per cent and 11 per cent of GDP in each country, respectively. In Norway, it took two years for the banking sector to return to profitability, and four years before bank lending was back to its pre-crisis level. In Sweden, return to profitability also took two years but it took 10 years before bank lending reached its pre-crisis level.

Norway: the Government Bank Investment Fund

In Norway, the banking industry privately funds two guarantee companies, the Savings Banks' Guarantee Funds and the Commercial Banks' Guarantee Fund. These were drawn down during the initial phase of the crisis (by 1991). In addition, several of the banks were merged and others were bankrupted and placed under temporary public administration.

The government initially started to fund the failed banks through its new Government Bank Insurance Fund in January 1991. This insurance fund was an independent legal entity with a mandate to provide liquidity to the two private guarantee funds. The fund was allowed to impose conditions both on the private funds and the banks receiving bail-out money. These conditions concerned, among other things, management issues such as hiring and firing of key personnel, board composition and major investment decisions.

The Norwegian government also implemented a division of labour between the Government Bank Insurance Fund and the Norwegian Central Bank. The former would channel support to banks that were largely insolvent while the latter would provide liquidity in the form of loans to largely solvent banks.

In the autumn of 1991, the crisis reached systemic proportions with large losses reported by the three largest commercial banks. These three banks held about half of the total assets in the banking sector.

At this point, the Norwegian parliament created a second financing vehicle: the Government Bank Investment Fund (GBIF). While the insurance fund continued to pour liquidity into insolvent banks, GBIF began to purchase securities floated by banks that were still relatively healthy. This included purchases of 'preferred capital', an equity-like contract that was convertible into common stock. In preparation for GBIF's purchase of this convertible preferred security, the Norwegian parliament amended the existing banking law, allowing the government to write down a bank's common stock to zero against its losses. The purpose of the amendment was to prevent equity holders from holding up (forcing bargaining with) the government as it proceeded to bail out the banking system.

66 Unlike Norway, Sweden issued a blanket guarantee of all bank loans in its banking system until July 1996 99

Subsequent common stock write-downs resulted in the GBIF becoming the sole owner of two of the three largest commercial banks, and the dominant owner of Den Norske Bank (DnB), the largest. By the end of the 1990s, the government had sold most of its banking shares to private investors, with the exception of a 'negative majority' (34 per cent) held in DnB. The negative majority allows the government to block a takeover – perhaps a benefit for some local interests but at the cost of reducing international competition for Norwegian banking assets.

The Norwegian economy started to recover in 1993 and the banking crisis was essentially over. Research at the Norwegian Central Bank indicates that, based largely on direct cash flows, the overall benefit of the government's intervention likely exceeded the direct cost (which included direct payments and interest rate subsidies) even without accounting for the value of various loan guarantees that never had to be called.

Sweden: the 'good bank/bad bank' model

The crisis in Sweden began with heavy losses reported by the country's largest savings bank, Första Sparbanken, in 1991. Later that year, the third-largest commercial bank (Nordbanken) also began reporting big losses. At the time, the Swedish government owned 71 per cent of the bank's common stock.

The government proceeded to purchase a new share issue and to buy out the private shareholders at the equity issue price. This was in contrast to Norway, where the private equity was forcibly written down to zero before the government proceeded to fund the bank.

In full control of Nordbanken, the government split the bank's assets into two parts: the 'good' assets were continued within the bank while the 'bad' non-performing loans were spun off into a separate legal entity called Securum, created in 1992. The spin-off into Securum was partly a response to Swedish banking regulations that prohibit banks from holding shares in the companies to which they lend money. Securum was not a bank, only an asset holding company and could, therefore, receive equity positions in the troubled companies when they defaulted on their bank debt.

A 'bad bank' solution was also created for Gota Bank, the fourth largest commercial bank, when it failed in early 1992. This time, the bad assets were transferred to Retriva, the asset management company. The remaining good assets of Gota Bank were auctioned off and eventually purchased by Nordbanken in 1993 with no payment to Gota Bank's shareholders.

Most of the troubled assets that Securum acquired from Nordbanken were in the form of loans to various financially distressed companies, with the remainder consisting largely of real estate holdings. Securum financed the purchase with the combination of a loan from Nordbanken and a government equity infusion. Securum's mission was to liquidate in an orderly fashion the troubled assets so as to maximise recovery. The management company was dissolved in 1997 after successfully liquidating its assets.

Securum drove a hard but successful bargain with many of its troubled borrowers. Part of the loan mass was by small companies, and it was not uncommon for the company founder or entrepreneur to pledge his own common stockholding in the company as collateral for the company's loan. If, however, the company failed to service the debt, Securum had the right to seize the pledged collateral, thus, in effect, acquiring control of the distressed company without the need for a formal bankruptcy procedure. In Sweden, the bankruptcy code mandates a quick auction sale of the bankrupt company (piecemeal or as a going concern).

Avoiding bankruptcy, Securum also avoided the auction time pressure, and instead proceeded to develop the troubled company in preparation for its sale as a going concern down the line. To support this strategy, Securum's management team was deliberately chosen to have industrial management experience, which contributed to its success.

Unlike Norway, Sweden also issued (in the autumn of 1992) a blanket guarantee of all bank loans in the Swedish banking system, effective until July 1996. Naturally, this blanket guarantee greatly benefited existing bank shareholders. Moreover, the Swedish Central Bank provided liquidity by depositing large foreign currency reserves in troubled banks, and by allowing banks to borrow freely the Swedish currency (at no risk to the central bank, given the government blanket loan guarantee). Perhaps because of these additional moves, the Swedish government's cash infusion to end the banking crisis was almost entirely limited to Nordbanken and Gota Bank.

In sum, both Sweden and Norway created bank restructuring agencies to oversee the government's cash infusion in troubled banks. Existing shareholders were largely forced out of the failed banks. Both countries also established strict guidelines for companies receiving government support, including balance sheet restructuring targets, risk management and cost cuts. Moreover, both countries engineered a public takeover of the largest troubled commercial banks, and promoted private bank mergers. However, only Sweden implemented a 'good bank/bad bank' model, and, perhaps most important, only Sweden issued a blanket creditor guarantee that greatly benefited existing bank shareholders. The end result was similar in both countries: a relatively speedy recovery and a return to robust economic growth. The macroeconomic impacts of these banking crises were relatively short-lived.

Lessons for the current downturn

When comparing Scandinavia with the US, what stands out is the role played by government ownership of the failed banks in Scandinavia. This role was (and still is) politically acceptable because the governments in Norway and Sweden have a long history of partnering with the private sector. Also, nepotism and outright corruption are minimal in these societies.

The US bail-out strategy up to the time of writing has been much less coherent, with a virtual case-by-case approach to the developing crisis. Thus, we have twice seen a specific loan guarantee to induce the takeover of a failed bank by a private party (JPMorgan's purchase of Bear Sterns, conditional on a $29bn government guarantee of Bear Stearns' debt; Bank of America's acquisition of Merrill Lynch with an initial assistance of $10bn from the Troubled Asset Relief Program); a cash infusion in return for a controlling equity position ($80bn paid to AIG in return for an 80 per cent equity stake in the insurance giant); cash infusions without taking back equity ($200bn to Fannie Mae and Freddie Mac after the twin mortgage companies were placed into federal 'conservatorship'; Tarp funds to nine banks, including $25bn to Citigroup); and auction purchases of non-performing loans from failing banks. As an extension of these policies, the US is also providing distressed loans to two industrial companies on the brink of bankruptcy (General Motors and Chrysler). Most recently, there is also talk about implementing a 'bad bank' solution to Citigroup's financial troubles, following the bank's write-offs of more than $90bn over the past five quarters. The plan is to spin off Citigroup's troubled businesses and assets into a separate entity (Citi Holdings) and gradually liquidate these over the next three years. This break-up plan comes after substantial cash infusions of Tarp funds.

In the US debate, government acquisition of controlling equity ownership positions in failed banks has proved to be controversial. Indeed, there remains a deeply rooted scepticism towards government ownership of private enterprise. However, as the Scandinavian experience suggests, the approach to this issue ought to be pragmatic. Since the objective is to maximise taxpayer returns from the bail-out, a greater commitment to government acquisition of equity stakes in troubled financial institutions ought to be considered. It is a zero-sum game: if the taxpayer does not insist on the best possible deal, some other party to the bail-out will reap benefits at the taxpayer's expense.

A clear case in point is the $8 per share windfall to shareholders of Bear Sterns, when the government debt guarantee of that bank caused JPMorgan to raise its takeover bid from $2 to $10. This type of shareholder windfall, which we also saw in Sweden as the stock market responded to the government's blanket debt guarantee, would have been avoided had the government taken an equity stake in the bailed-out bank.

5

Japan: Hubris, denial and the loss of confidence

Financial collapse dealt Japan a shock from which it has yet to fully recover. By **Jean-Pierre Lehmann**

Twenty years ago, though the term did not exist as such, there was a 'Tokyo consensus' reflected in a series of Japanese phrases that became part of universal business jargon: *gyosei shido* (administrative guidance), whereby the all-powerful Ministry of International Trade and Industry picked winners among sectors and companies and, thus, drove Japan to ever higher competitiveness; *keiretsu* (industrial groups), whereby Japanese companies were joined by various financial and managerial links, thus achieving both horizontal and vertical integration; *kanban* (just in time), whereby Japanese manufacturers obtained parts directly from suppliers and sub-contractors that were immediately installed on the assembly line, hence abolishing inventory and greatly enhancing productivity; and *kaizen* (continuous improvement), whereby all members of the 'corporate family' participate in multiple improvements, no matter how seemingly small.

During the 1980s, when Japan's gross domestic product was recording very high growth, a monumental asset inflation was occurring. As the stock market and real estate prices soared, interest rates were kept very low, banks provided ample and easy credit and companies invested continuously, especially in construction, resulting in massive loans and overcapacity. Then the bubble burst. The stock market and real estate prices crashed and the banks were faced with mountains of bad loans.

Furthermore, during these years, Japanese industry continued to rely on existing strengths, with very little innovation to meet the new challenges of globalisation, information technology and the services revolution and, thus, to act as growth engines. There are some very strong companies in Japan that weathered the crisis, but they are in traditional sectors such as automotive (Toyota and Honda) or electronic office equipment (Canon) rather than in what might be termed 21st-century leading sectors. Japan remains especially weak in services. Consequently, the state of its economy remains highly dependent on exports.

There is one striking similarity between the Japanese crisis and the current downturn: the hubris that preceded them. The Japanese were convinced the sun would shine, if not forever, at least for a long, long time. And that conviction, in turn, was buttressed by a belief that the superiority of the Japanese system was culturally innate.

Japan's mistakes

The differences between the US and Japan are too numerous to enumerate here. One important difference in the context of their reciprocal crises lies in consumer behaviour: Americans are the world's biggest spenders while the Japanese are among the world's biggest savers. Profligacy, however, featured in the preludes to both crises.

In the course of the second half of the 1980s, corporate Japan went on an investment spree, both domestically and internationally. With interest rates low and the yen having doubled in value against the dollar following the September 1985 Plaza Accord, which resulted in the depreciation of the dollar in relation to the yen, foreign assets seemed especially cheap. Hence, the frenzy in buying mainly US, but also European and Australian, high-prestige real estate (Rockefeller Centre in New York), golf courses (Pebble Beach in California) and companies (Columbia Pictures film studio).

> During the 1980s, when Japan's GDP growth was very high, a monumental asset inflation was occurring

This era of intoxication also saw the extravagant purchase of numerous works of art, notably Vincent van Gogh's 'Vase with Fifteen Sunflowers' by Yasuo Goto, a Japanese insurance magnate, for almost $40m in 1987, a record at the time.

Japanese institutions also invested heavily in the domestic real estate market, with the result that, as pundits were fond of pointing out at the time, the value of the land surrounding the Imperial Palace in Tokyo was greater than that of the entire state of California.

When the bubble burst in 1991, the Japanese financial market was hit by a tsunami of bad loans and many institutions, including some of the most venerable, such as LTCB (Long-Term Credit Bank) and Yamaichi Securities, collapsed.

Unlike the US, in Japan the profligacy was almost entirely institutional. Japan has never had a well-developed consumer culture and the reforms that might have been undertaken at the time to create one did not materialise. The country retained its fundamentally closed form of bureaucracy-controlled corporatist capitalism. When the government sought to combat deflation and re-boot the economy by boosting consumer demand – including by literally dishing out cash – it failed. Japan's few apparent bouts of recovery were invariably caused by external forces, notably growth in exports to China.

Perhaps Japan's biggest failing was the long period during which officials and opinion leaders remained in a state of denial. The hubris had been such that the possibilities of fundamental weaknesses in the system were rejected.

Two very different events in 1995 woke Japan from complacency to a state of calamity. On January 17, the Kobe earthquake killed 6,500 people. The shock of the human tragedy was compounded by the government's floundering incompetence in responding, resulting in far more deaths and destruction than there should have been. The myth of all-knowing Japanese officialdom was instantly destroyed and has never recovered.

The second event was the sarin gas attack on the Tokyo metro on March 20, when Aum-Shinrikyo, a terrorist sect, killed 12 people and injured 5,500. Japan's self-image as the quintessential land of security and social harmony was punctured.

The financial crisis, the protracted state of denial and the two calamitous events of 1995 shattered the confidence of the Japanese people. That confidence has never been restored and seems unlikely, on the basis of current political, economic, social and demographic trends, to be restored in the foreseeable future.

Lessons for the current downturn

Japan's socio-economic model differs great from that of other countries but there are lessons to be drawn. Three in particular stand out:

■ What goes up must eventually come down. When the sun is shining, prepare for rainy days for they will come. One of the key lessons from Japan's crisis is that of humility.

■ Japan's experience illustrates the terrible consequences of loss of confidence. At times of crisis, confidence is the most important force to restore.

■ The crisis could have been turned into a massive opportunity had 'Fortress Japan' opened up. It did not. The one thing that could transform the US financial crisis into a global drama would be if the US were to emulate Japan and become closed.

chapter

Seizing the upside of a downturn

Managers who see economic strife only as a threat are missing out on an ideal opportunity to implement change and instil better practice. By **Donald Sull**

In a downturn, most managers fixate on the abundant bad news: demand is down, prices are falling, credit is scarce, and lay-offs are likely. Obsessing over threats obscures a surprising but crucial truth about downturns: the worst of times for the economy as a whole can be the best of times for individual firms to create value for the long term.

In past downturns, some companies, including Toyota, Nokia, Cisco, Samsung and Emirates, emerged from an economic crisis stronger than before. Like the mythological Libyan wrestler Antaeus who regained strength when thrown to the ground, these companies derived strength from economic hard times. Many of their competitors, in contrast, languished or failed. Part of the difference is down to having managers who understand how to create value during a downturn, as well as their effectiveness in acting on these insights.

Every downturn opens a window of opportunity to adjust the status quo, and astute managers push through necessary changes while the window is open. An economic crisis marks a sharp break with the past, and, observing the break, employees recognise that a firm cannot continue to do what it did in the past. The downturn lowers their resistance to change and cuts through complacency. A downturn often brings latent challenges to a head, and savvy managers can harness the resulting energy to infuse the organisation with a sense of urgency in fixing these problems.

A downturn provides a ready-made external rationale to justify painful decisions that would appear extreme in better times. Finally, an economic crisis provides managers with air cover to make decisions that incur short-term financial pain for long-term gain, such as pruning products, 'firing' unprofitable customers or exiting money-losing businesses. Investors, boards and bosses are typically more forgiving of short-term dips in sales and earnings during a downturn, when all competitors are suffering, than they are during a boom, when everyone else is thriving.

Managers can harness a downturn to make any number of possible changes, but the following four actions in particular are likely to create long-term value.

Instil ongoing cost discipline

During the boom years, many managers thought their objective was to increase revenues through innovation. It is not. Companies exist to create economic value, which is the difference between revenues and the opportunity cost of all inputs (including capital). Good managers keep their hands on both levers at all times, looking for growth opportunities during downturns while maintaining cost discipline when the good times roll.

Unfortunately, best practice is not common practice. Many companies veer between periods of undisciplined growth and brutal cost cutting. During a boom, they press on the gas pedal to increase revenues. When the economic cycle turns, however, they slam on the brakes, abandon growth and focus on slashing expenses to free cash flow. Once the economy picks up again, they abandon their new-found cost discipline to pursue revenue growth.

" Most managers look for golden opportunities when the good times are rolling. This is a mistake. The best ones often arise during downturns "

This stop-go approach is a mistake. Golden opportunities to increase sales often emerge in downturns (see below). The best opportunities to cut costs often arise in good times. During a boom, managers tend to overlook the inefficiencies that sprout like weeds throughout the organisation, sapping resources from more productive uses. During a downturn, good managers weed their overgrown gardens, but great ones also build processes to nip these costs in the bud as they crop up in the future.

Toyota overtook its Detroit rivals in large part through its 'lean' production system, which continuously reduces costs by identifying and eliminating activities or materials that do not add value for end users. The carmaker pioneered these processes not in benign markets, but in 1950 during a deep downturn that depressed automobile demand and forced most Japanese automakers into the red.

Toyota managers did not ask what to cut, but addressed the more fundamental question of how to systematically identify and eliminate waste on an ongoing basis. Teams of managers benchmarked best practices within Toyota, and discovered an experimental process within the company's own machine shop, where successive work stations took only the parts or materials they needed at that point in time. This minimised inventories and quickly identified problems along the assembly line.

In instilling these processes, Toyota did several things well. First, managers looked outside the company for ideas without slavishly following the latest management fads. Second, they continued to refine their processes and added complementary practices including visual signals to pull more inventory and a system that allowed workers to stop the assembly line when they detected a problem.

Third, they used the downturn to negotiate changes in work practices. The Toyota system required workers to man more machines, provide constant suggestions for improvement and move among stations as work flow dictated. The downturn helped convince workers that these changes were necessary. Fourth, managers recognised that no company is an island, but is embedded in an ecosystem of suppliers and distributors, and they extended these practices to their suppliers. Finally, the company continued to use and improve these processes when the market picked up.

Managers can look for ways to build ongoing discipline into resource allocation processes. In many companies, the budgeting process takes the previous year's expenditures as given, and then incrementally augments or decreases them to calculate the next year's budget. Facing a deep recession in Brazil in 1983, retailer Lojas Americanas introduced zero-based budgeting that required managers to develop budgets from scratch and justify each item.

To instil ongoing cost discipline, managers should ask themselves a few questions. What processes do we have in place to systematically identify and eliminate waste? Could we improve these procedures? Are there promising best practices in parts of our organisation that we could disseminate more widely?

Force hard choices

Good times produce ample resources that blunt the need to make hard trade-offs. During a boom, managers tend to spread resources evenly to preserve a sense of fairness and minimise conflict. Even in the best of times, this means that promising opportunities receive fewer resources than they require while others get more than they deserve.

In the worst of times, it is even more harmful, dissipating scarce cash. Many managers, for example, try to spread the pain of downsizing evenly, demanding an identical percentage reduction in headcount or expenditure across all units regardless of their merits.

A downturn provides the ideal opportunity to force hard choices. Consider Nokia. After the Soviet Union crumbled in the early 1990s, Finland suffered one of the worst recessions in its history, and Nokia, then a diversified conglomerate, faced financial distress. Rather than spreading cuts evenly, Nokia's executives made the hard call to focus on the fledgling telecommunications business while exiting other businesses that then accounted for nearly 90 per cent of revenues.

This example illustrates important points about making hard choices during a downturn. First, managers must be willing to reverse their previous decisions. During the 1980s, Nokia executives invested heavily in consumer electronics, but when that bet failed to pay off, the top team was willing to cut their losses and focus on the much smaller mobile phone business. Second, Nokia's executives recognised that betting on telecommunications reduced the group's diversification and exposed the focused firm to greater risk. They offset this with other risk management tools, including diversification within telecommunications (for example, handsets and infrastructure), spreading across geographic markets and achieving economies of scale.

A downturn provides an occasion to make hard choices not only in the C-suite, but throughout the organisation. After the dotcom bubble burst in 2001, Cisco suffered a sharp decline in sales. The company's leadership responded by forcing hard choices at every level, including consolidating suppliers from 1,300 to 420, halving the number of channel partners, culling the bottom third of products, streamlining research and development projects and sharply reducing acquisitions.

During the boom, Cisco middle managers enjoyed wide latitude to acquire start-ups – the company snapped up two dozen in 2000 alone.

During the downturn, Cisco tightened up the process by creating an investment review board that met monthly to vet acquisition targets. Managers proposing acquisitions were required to draw up detailed integration plans and personally commit to hitting sales and earnings targets for the new business.

Companies can also harness a downturn to prioritise which corporate initiatives really matter. Corporate 'priorities' tend to proliferate during a boom. Middle managers in one European engineering group counted more than 50 so-called 'strategic priorities' that had rained down on them from headquarters during the preceding two years. This excess of objectives consumes not only cash, but also diverts managerial attention from what truly matters.

In a downturn, senior executives should consolidate their major initiatives into a single list and select a handful that are truly critical. To ensure everyone gets the message, they should communicate the key priorities throughout the entire organisation, including a list of initiatives that are no longer objectives. Senior executives can give these priorities teeth by eliminating key performance indicators linked to less critical initiatives and link the bonuses of managers to corporate objectives.

To force hard choices, managers can ask themselves a series of questions. What initiatives, businesses, products, markets and so on, have a call on our scarce resources? Can we rank order them in terms of value creation potential? Where should we draw the line that marks the truly critical from the nice to have?

Accelerate fundamental changes

Prior to the current downturn, many organisations embarked upon large-scale change programmes. Common examples include shifting from selling products to services, fostering greater collaboration across organisational silos, or building a more entrepreneurial culture. Major change efforts are difficult in the best of times, and many executives worry that a downturn will halt future progress or reverse any gains made to date. Indeed, in a downturn, managers too often scurry from fighting one fire to the next and thereby lose sight of the longer transformation effort.

Large-scale change initiatives typically require eight to 10 years to complete and often run out of steam along the way. Downturns provide an ideal opportunity to re-invigorate an ongoing transformation. Managers can harness a downturn to renew a sense of urgency, justify unpopular decisions and overcome complacency or resistance to change.

The case of Samsung illustrates this. After succeeding his father as Samsung Group chairman in 1987, Lee Kun-hee launched a programme to transform the conglomerate from a good Korean competitor to a great global group. Fifteen years later, Samsung Electronics, the group's flagship business, had largely achieved this ambition, leading in technological innovation, market share of key products, brand awareness, and financial returns. A careful analysis of Samsung's transformation reveals that most of the critical decisions that propelled the group were concentrated during two downturns.

After a promising start in the mid-1980s, Samsung's transformation was running out of steam. Mr Lee used the global recession during the early 1990s to force through a series of difficult changes in short order. He divested businesses, such as sugar and paper processing, that had a profitable and long-standing place in the group's portfolio, because they could not achieve leadership in global markets.

Mr Lee concentrated research and development and advertising expenditures on a handful of businesses deemed capable of competing globally while curtailing expenditures in others. He insisted that subsidiaries measure performance against global leaders, rather than benchmark other Korean companies, and instituted manufacturing processes to produce world-class quality. Finally, Mr Lee bucked the Korean tradition of basing promotions strictly on seniority to advance a large number of young executives based on their performance and global outlook.

By the mid-1990s, Mr Lee was concerned that the transformation was losing traction. While other Korean executives bemoaned the Asian Economic crisis beginning in 1997, Mr Lee saw it as another opportunity to re-invigorate Samsung's transformation. He divested additional units and led a further round of headcount reductions. He also increased the autonomy of the remaining businesses by eliminating cross-business subsidies, loan guarantees and below-market transfer prices. These changes, which marked a sharp break from traditional Korean business practices, freed Samsung to compete more effectively in global markets.

As they enter the fray of short-term retrenchment, managers should ask themselves these questions to keep sight of long-term transformation. Which large-scale changes did we start prior to the downturn? Which do we still consider critical to our long-term success? What changes would we have to make even if this crisis had never occurred? How can we harness the crisis to accelerate these changes?

Seize golden opportunities

Golden opportunities refer to occasions when a company can create value significantly in excess of the cost of the resources required to seize the opportunity. Examples include acquisitions at bargain prices (think Santander's acquisition of Alliance & Leicester and Bradford & Bingley); innovative products, such as Apple's iPod, that dominate a new sector; expanding in emerging markets; or acquiring valuable resources cheaply.

Most managers look for golden opportunities when the good times are rolling. This is a mistake. The best opportunities often arise during downturns when distressed sellers are forced to offload valuable assets at bargain prices – recall how ING Direct snapped up the deposits unloaded by failing Icelandic banks. To conserve cash, companies may be forced to retreat from attractive propositions, thereby creating an opportunity for rivals. In the face of the current recession, Adobe Systems may scale back its ambitions in web-design software, creating an opening for a deep-pocket competitor such as Microsoft.

> **Managers can harness a downturn to renew a sense of urgency, justify unpopular decisions and overcome complacency**

Competitors may have to pass on new opportunities to conserve cash. Airbus launched its A380 into the industry downturn following the terrorist attacks of September 11 2001 when few airlines had the wherewithal to buy the new aircraft despite its greater range, size and fuel efficiency. Emirates, in contrast, pounced.

Sometimes, seizing the opportunity requires a creative deal to help ease another company's pain. When the South Korean won collapsed during the Asian crisis in the late 1990s, Korean producers flooded the European market with cheap microwave ovens, driving European appliance makers near bankruptcy. The Chinese company Guangdong Galanz negotiated a novel agreement with European white goods companies. The Europeans moved their state-of-the-art production lines to China, where Galanz manufactured microwaves for half the cost, and secured the right to use the spare manufacturing capacity to make its microwaves for sale in Asia. Galanz thereby secured cutting-edge manufacturing technology, economies of scale, and exposure to leading companies' product design, which allowed it to quickly emerge as the world's largest producer of microwaves.

In a downturn, it is easy for managers to focus exclusively on managing threats, and thereby lose sight of golden opportunities. To counter-balance this, they should ask themselves the following questions. Are competitors retreating from opportunities that we can seize? Should we double down in growth markets, such as Bric economies, rather than retrenching to our core? Does our customers' or competitors' pain create an opportunity for us? Can we snap up key resources at bargain prices?

All the economic bad news can eclipse the crucial reality that every downturn has an upside. To make the most of that upside, managers must recognise opportunities during hard times and muster the courage to seize them.

7

Managing fluctuations

Managers who see economic strife only as a threat are missing out on an ideal opportunity. By **Andrew Scott**

M ost businesses are busy during the day but close down in the evening. On a Friday evening, the economy enters a severe contraction only to emerge into a boom on Monday morning. After the Christmas and New Year holidays, the economy shifts from boom into a deep recession. Arranging costs and employment to minimise the effects of these fluctuations is a daily task for managers. Further, the size of these fluctuations is enormous compared with the volatility of business cycles and yet companies seem to find business cycle recessions particularly painful.

Corporate anxiety about recessions has two sources. First, concern over how deep the fall in gross domestic product will be; and second, uncertainty over how long the slowdown will last. It is this second factor that makes recessions so difficult for companies. While retailers can never be sure how big their Christmas surge will be, they do at least know when it occurs and how long it will last. Although economic forecasts abound, no one can reliably pronounce on the duration of the current downturn.

Not knowing the depth or length of this recession leaves companies in a situation similar to wearing a blindfold while twisting and turning on the down part of a rollercoaster – a sense of panic and fear grips the imagination combined with an intense focus on just surviving the moment. This urge to focus on survival is important but smart companies do much more during a downturn. They realise that steps taken now to boost performance lay the foundations for future success. Also, rather than just focusing on the horror of the current moment and marvelling at its historical uniqueness, they can review past recessions to assess what makes a good strategy.

This need to focus not just on survival but also on the next upturn is important. Just as the weekend is shorter than the week, so recessions are normally shorter than expansions. In the 20th century, the average US contraction lasted just over 14 months while the average expansion lasted slightly more than four and a half years. Measures taken in a downturn will serve as the basis for success in an upturn. Some economists even argue that a recession acts as a 'pitstop' – a time when a company retunes and re-optimises, raising productivity, making acquisitions and ensuring even better performance when the good times roll again.

When order books are full, it is an expensive time to shut production, reorganise and allocate management time to internal issues. However, in a downturn, with resources lying idle, the opportunity cost of investing in organisational capital, such as workplace practices, and in a company's human capital, improving and retraining the workforce, falls. As a result, productivity tends to rise during a recession. Added incentive to raise productivity comes from the sharper competitive pressures of a downturn. With this recession characterised by a sharp credit crunch, the concept of investing in a company's intangible capital, which is usually not cash intensive, has added attractiveness.

> ❝ In a downturn the opportunity cost of investing in organisational capital falls, so productivity tends to rise during a recession ❞

A further standard feature of recessions is an increase in the diversity of company performance. While economists talk of the cleansing effects of recessions, it is not only poor companies that face the risk of extinction. In fact, there is a surprisingly low correlation between the profit performance of companies before a recession and bankruptcy. This raises another opportunity for companies during a downturn – mergers and acquisitions.

Although the returns to M&A activity are notoriously weak, even possibly negative, these facts suggest that buying during a downturn may be the most likely way of providing shareholders value for money. Of course, in a credit crunch the problem is financing M&A, although an unusual feature of this downturn is the health of corporate balances. It is companies in the household and financial sector which, on average, find themselves with high debt and who are trying to deleverage rapidly. Of course, only the average corporate balance sheet looks better than normal for this stage of the business cycle. That average will hide very high leverage among some companies who will be hard hit by the credit crunch. However, this diversity only provides further scope for M&A deals.

Is this recession different from past downturns?

So far, we have focused on what usually happens during a recession and there is no doubt that companies can learn much from these episodes. But how does this recession differ from pervious ones? And what does this mean for companies?

The first main difference is its likely duration. In the US, the National Bureau of Economic Research dates recession as beginning in December 2007. It is, therefore, already the third longest recession since 1945 and if it survives until May it will become the longest postwar recession. The longer it lasts, the harder it will be to survive, and the less relevant the metaphor of a pitstop will become.

There seem to be three likely scenarios. The first and most optimistic is that recession ends in the second half of 2009 as a result of the substantial actions of governments in reducing interest rates, shoring up the banking system and raising government deficits. The second is that recession continues throughout 2009 and recovery occurs in 2010, but only weakly, and the economy follows the anaemic experience of Japan during the past decade. The third and most terrifying possibility is of a continued pronounced downturn similar to the Great Depression of the 1930s. From a risk management perspective, companies need to assess how exposed they are to each of these scenarios.

The difficulty is that in the next six months it is likely to be impossible to determine which of these paths is unfolding. The economic news is likely to be remorselessly bad in all cases, with further dramatic government intervention to be expected. However, across all three scenarios the same focus on internal efficiency drives, restructuring and retraining and improving the quality of the match between each post and each worker is critical.

What does differ is the immediacy of any M&A activity. Once there are signs of recovery, business optimism changes dramatically and opportunities disappear almost as rapidly. The blindfolded rollercoaster rider fears that there is still further to go, but as soon as upward momentum is detected, anxieties and apprehensions disappear and past concerns are forgotten. The same is true for asset markets and acquisitions. But if we face a prolonged period of weak growth or even further falls in GDP beyond 2009, then acquiring companies today will regret not delaying acquisitions until later.

The second feature of this recession is the way it is focused on those who have been reliant on credit and the way it has hit hardest the financial and real estate sector. Any individual, company or country that has these characteristics will be hit the hardest. Another striking feature of this downturn is how badly the effect on consumption will be. Normally in a downturn, it is investment that takes the hit but this time round it looks like consumption will suffer much more than usual. The effect on the retail sector is obvious.

In a recession, business horizons tend to shrink and survival becomes paramount. Yet preparing for the next good times, whenever they may be, is also important. It is important to try and anticipate how the next set of good times will differ from the last expansion. Recessions are, therefore, a time to make long-term bets – which is presumably why the US auto industry has declared its intention to focus on greener technologies.

What can we say about the next expansion? Forecasts are inevitably speculative but some factors seem to be taking shape. The first is a rise of government regulation. As a result of environmental issues and in response to globalisation, governments have recently increased regulatory controls. The enormous intervention in the financial system, and a general zeitgeist that markets cannot be relied upon, will embolden governments further. This may even put at risk some of the past gains of globalisation.

In addition, either through regulation or impaired balance sheets, it seems unlikely that leverage will be so high in the next expansion, which suggests an increase in the real cost of capital. This will be further exacerbated by higher risk premiums – the 'Great Moderation' has been rudely interrupted and financial markets will once again be concerned about risk. Once recovery sets in, inflation expectations are also likely to be higher than during the previous expansion. Lastly, during a severe downturn, with employment rising rapidly, governments will be more likely to approve mergers with anti-competitive aspects. The consequence is that the next upturn is less likely to be characterised by strong competition.

The last expansion saw tremendous growth in the financial sector, with rising wages and employment. Many of the brightest young minds were drawn into this sector, but it now seems that the financial sector is destined to be smaller. This can only be beneficial for other sectors as the war for talent eases. This brings us back to my earlier theme. Investments made in the downturn will have a shaping influence on success in the next upturn. Key among these investments will be investing in the next generation of senior managers. Some of these are currently out of employment and looking for a new career.

" Companies need to focus not just on survival but also on the upturn. Investments made in the downturn will shape success in the recovery "

Recessions are bad for business, yet companies are used to dealing with fluctuations. This recession is bad, in fact unusually bad. Merely surviving it will be a big corporate challenge. However, downturns also present opportunities that companies should take to restructure, reorganise and invest in plans for the future. Internal reforms, better job-worker matching, training and key recruitment and possible M&A should be high on the agenda. Focusing on the horrors of survival is no way to prepare for future upturns – fluctuations have to be managed and anticipated. Companies that were not sufficiently prepared for this downturn should have learnt their lesson – prepare now for the next upturn.

8

Death of the decoupling myth

In the era of globalisation, the idea of decoupling is dead. By **Suzanne Rosselet-McCauley**

T he questions remain: how deep will it be and how long will it last? Will some countries come out stronger while others tilt into bankruptcy? A global economic meltdown will have consequences for national competitiveness, which the IMD World Competitiveness Center defines as how a state manages its path to prosperity. This is a concept that not only encompasses economic performance, but also the impact on the environment, on quality of life and on economic and social infrastructures.

Global economic growth is estimated to fall to 0.5 per cent this year, down from 3.7 per cent last year and 5 per cent in 2007. Any global gross domestic product growth of less than 3 per cent generally implies a world recession, even if that does not mean that all countries are in decline. The majority of the rich industrialised countries have now entered a recessionary period and the emerging economies, which grew on average 7 to 8 per cent during the past few years, could slow to 3.3 per cent. Growth will be driven mainly by developing Asia. Compared with the contraction in growth of the rich industrialised economies, the developing economies may be better shielded from the global turmoil. But they will feel the pain as the world's economic engines falter.

In this era of globalisation, with almost all countries integrated into the global economy, the decoupling myth is dead. The emerging markets of China, Brazil, India and others will not be insulated from the downturn in the US and Europe, as many people were predicting six months ago. In fact, the financial crisis is turning out to be much deeper and broader than expected.

In the worst-case scenario, emerging economies will suffer their own full-blown crises. The most vulnerable are those countries and regions that depended heavily on foreign capital (including Hungary, the Baltic states, Turkey, central Asia), or those that have big current account deficits, but all are seeing their credit drying up. Export-dependent nations such as Japan, Germany, South Korea and China will suffer from the contraction in global demand and can only turn towards their own domestic markets or neighbours to pick up the slack.

" Emerging markets will not be insulated from the downturn "

Many economies are witnessing huge wealth destruction due to falling property values and stock market crashes. The domino effect began with the US subprime mortgage crisis, followed by the UK, Spain and Ireland. Germany and Japan are the most recent victims to fall into recession. The knock-on effects have been felt as far away as Kazakhstan. China has also been hit hard, since many people invested life savings in the stock market and small and medium-sized enterprises are particularly suffering from the credit squeeze.

Tightening credit conditions are also having an effect on consumer spending all over the world. Banks have significantly cut back on their lending and the world's economies are deteriorating dramatically as banks, companies and households cling more tightly to cash, despite the aggressive loosening of monetary policy and generous fiscal measures. Interest rates are approaching zero in the US, the Bank of England has lowered interest rates to 1.5 per cent, the lowest since its foundation in 1694, and the European Central Bank recently cut rates to 2.5 per cent. Rates are expected to be slashed even further. When standard monetary policy responses reach their limit, fiscal options, such as cutting taxes and increasing public spending, come into play. The only good news is the drop in inflation rates across the world.

The US, Japan, the European Union and China have all spent hundreds of billions of dollars to stimulate the economy. But is there any money left? The US recently passed the $10,000bn debt milestone – there was not enough space on the national debt clock in New York City to display the 13 zeros. The UK is particularly vulnerable, with its high level of household indebtedness (150 per cent of disposable income, one of the highest in the developed world) and a high dependency on the financial sector for jobs. The sector accounts for more than one-fifth of all UK employment, compared with only 6 per cent of jobs in the US, and contributed about 25 per cent of the nation's economic growth in the past five years. However, the financial sector only contributes about 8 per cent to UK GDP and the services sector remains very dynamic. Consequently, this long-term investment in innovative and, hopefully, adaptable services industries should enable the UK to weather the current turbulence and to emerge stronger in competitiveness after the downturn. Nevertheless, the financial sector will require improved governance that will entail more effective regulation.

Japan's government debt amounts to more than 170 per cent of its GDP. In Italy it is more than 100 per cent. Spain and Greece are not far behind. And with the exception of Germany, every large industrial economy will run a big budget deficit in 2009. To some extent, government budgets in rich countries have automatic stabilisers to smooth out economic cycles between booms and busts. But in this crisis of a lifetime, these highly indebted countries could see their monetary and fiscal options limited.

> **Large industrial economies will run a big budget deficit in 2009. Japan's government debt stands at more than 170% of it GDP**

And big budget deficits and high debt place a heavy burden on future generations. These countries may be looking at a long tunnel of stagnation and vicious debt spiral, suggesting a bleak outlook for their competitiveness.

Surplus countries such as China, Russia and the Gulf states have accumulated enormous reserves via sovereign wealth funds. But the impact of the financial crisis could see a drawing-down of reserves as central banks ride to the rescue of credit-starved banks and companies. Sovereign wealth funds have quickly lost their enthusiasm for bailing out distressed US and European financial institutions. Many governments may now wish to access those reserves, which were saved up for such 'rainy days'. Apart from Russia and perhaps Brazil, these surplus countries may pull through this crisis with less damage than those that did not invest sufficiently in their future competitiveness. This means greater diversification of economic activities and investment in social infrastructure, especially in education.

Many of the world's developing countries will most likely suffer declines in competitiveness due to weakening exports and the drying up of capital. Those in the most dire of straits, such as Hungary, may be rescued by the IMF or may receive funding from cash-rich countries. But in order to reap long-term gains in prosperity, these countries need to increasingly focus on driving their domestic demand and counting less on foreign capital for growth. Sustainability of competitiveness will also depend on how well these countries adopt international best practices of corporate governance, transparency, fair and flexible labour legislation, environmental protection and a stronger societal framework.

There may be winning nations that will find the 'right' recipe for growth and competitiveness despite a climate of increased uncertainty and confusion. But it is too soon to make any significant forecasts. The US may prove more resilient than expected. Martin Wolf, the FT's chief economics commentator, once wrote, 'We Europeans are always gloomy about our successes, while the Americans are always optimistic about their failures'. But this will also depend on how long the recession lasts and what form it takes: a 'V', short but already discounted; a 'W' or double-dip; or the worst-case 'L' that could last much longer.

We may see a historic opportunity for the world's most important economies to show a united front in the face of this global crisis. Last year's G20 summit meeting in Washington implied the shift in the balance of economic power to be more inclusive of emerging nations. If the advanced and emerging economies can agree to co-operate and commit to stimulating the world economy and avoid protectionism, this could signal greater openness of the world economy. The consequences would be gains in competitiveness for those countries that decide to 'stick together rather than hang together' as Helmut Schmidt, the former German chancellor was fond of saying. These countries could emerge healthier from the global slowdown and benefit from greater sustainability of competitiveness.

Getting through the crisis

9

Fortune favours the well-prepared

Managing risk means being able and ready to adapt, not just following mathematical models and industry best practice. By **Russell Walker**

Traditionally, organisations have viewed risk management as a corporate requirement, and have often grouped it with audit and regulatory functions. Some have even empowered and titled corporate groups to 'manage risk' along these lines. This has often centred on managing insurance policies and reviewing reports from rating agencies, which suggests that risk management was viewed more as the hedging of certain risks and the overall outsourcing of critical risk analysis, especially as related to credit risk.

The recent economic downturn has shown a new face and place for risk management. The strongest companies in this downturn are those that integrated risk management as a more comprehensive part of corporate strategy. The weaker companies depended on the traditional risk management school of thought mentioned above almost entirely. This is true in financial services and extends to nearly all industries reliant on credit, market, and operational risk management.

As a result, a few key behaviours of risk management as a driver of corporate strategy have emerged. First and foremost, sound risk management requires executive involvement and ownership. Next, a culture and climate must exist for openly communicating risk in the organisation. Additionally, communication of risk must have an emphasis on data-driven decisions. Last, but perhaps most critically, the organisation must have a 'ready response' to a known risk.

Let us look first at how executive involvement in risk management helps to make it part of corporate strategy. A good example is US bank JPMorgan Chase, which has avoided the worst woes afflicting its competitors and has brilliantly executed a strategy that is rooted in understanding its risk and adapting as required. Witness its buying of Bear Stearns, the US investment bank, at $10 a share and its purchase of Washington Mutual, formerly the largest savings and loans operator in the US.

Unlike many of his peers, Jamie Dimon, JPMorgan chairman and chief executive, takes an active role in regular risk briefings. Not only does he ask for detailed risk reports, he also recognises the need to set a direction for the company in reaction to these risk outlooks rather than delegating the risk decisions. When the investment banking industry was moving towards greater real-estate investments and larger collateralised debt obligations purchases, he looked to data from the JPMorgan retail banks that showed that mortgage defaults were on the rise, and then provided his team the direction (based on data) to move against the herd by selling real-estate backed securities. It is hard to fathom that any organisation would make such a drastic decision about risk without the direct involvement of its senior leadership. So, just as executive involvement is important in setting corporate strategy, it is equally important in risk decisions.

To be effective as an organisation, there must be honesty and openness in communicating risks. It is clear that the international real-estate bubble was in part fuelled by a field of mortgages that were, in various forms, deceitful, incomplete or otherwise untraditional. Indeed, the classically trained credit risk managers signalled these mortgages as high risks. For many organisations that were focused on short-term earnings and felt a need to outpace the industry in bookings, this communication of risk was dismissed, or worse, silenced.

In the case of JPMorgan, it was the retail banking division that shared data with the investment bank on the escalations in mortgage delinquencies. This sharing of data across business lines allowed Mr Dimon and his corporate team to change strategy on the investment side. For many organisations, sharing information that challenges accepted norms or questions conventional wisdom is not welcomed. Other banks could have done the same as JPMorgan, but the practice of communicating risks and data across business lines was absent. The lesson, of course, is that an enterprise must be willing to communicate about risk, especially when things are going well and the risk has yet to be realised. Given the interconnectedness of risk within an organisation, all lines should take the time to learn what other lines are doing.

The importance of information in risk management should not be missed. In recent months, many risk managers have pondered how the traditional risk management models failed to predict the crisis. After all, a great deal of thought has gone into the development of the models and techniques that are used to conventionally manage risk. But it is in the convention that the problem resides.

Conventional risk management techniques use historical data to make projections about 'worse cases' or statistical anomalies that might arise. However, future negative outcomes are unknown to the models and future 'failure paths' are not incorporated into the models. Most of the risk models used are not good at incorporating new information and even worse at new types or sources of information, such as changes observed in a tangential business line, observations from front-line staff or traders, or alternations in market behaviour due to phenomena such as reduced availability of capital.

When JPMorgan saw signs in its mortgage accounts, it incorporated information on mortgage payments that was unconventional for the evaluation of portfolios of mortgages by the investment bank. Its success came from identifying such novel information and realising that it challenged conventional thinking. In such conditions, relying on conventional risk models is highly questionable – some would even say harmful. So, the focus of a risk manager should not be strictly quantification, but the identification and incorporation of information, especially of new types and new sources, in order to determine direction and the changes that drive risk. Risk management is inherently a process of investigation and learning that is rooted in unravelling the complexity of the unknown.

❝❝ JPMorgan's success came from identifying novel data and realising that it challenged conventional thinking ❞❞

The risks facing organisations are more complex and tightly connected than ever before. This complexity is largely driven by the ongoing globalisation of business and the increased speed of business activity, as enabled by technological advances. Using data to make decisions is key; it enables verification, and provides a means of breaking down the complexity of business.

For many organisations, there was a reliance on securitisation or swaps to transfer risk in ways that were not possible a few years previously. In many ways, these swaps served as insurance, yet the buyers of such swaps were not necessarily qualified or even financially guaranteed (as is required by many insurers worldwide). It is clear that very few of the buyers or sellers of such novel financial instruments understood the inherent interconnectedness of risks in these instruments.

For instance, the US government is still unwinding the trades and obligations of AIG, the insurance group, which relied heavily on swaps and risk transfers. The case of AIG shows how even a large and diversified company can struggle to fully understand its obligations and risks. Many companies relied heavily on hedging or transferring risk as a means of risk management. The assumption that risk is perfectly transferred assumes that the counterparty is perfectly resilient, too. This is, of course, naïve and has been proved wrong recently, but it demonstrates how a few assumptions about risk can drastically impede a corporate strategy.

Nevertheless, in every corporate strategy, particular risks are accepted, ideally those risks that management believes hold some attractive opportunity. Focusing on the data or factors that foretell of the risk accepted is essential; it is how one begins to understand a risk and reduce uncertainty. Risk management is a process of investigation and study.

However, many companies have accepted data at face value, such as credit ratings, the financial stability of a counterparty that was buying a swap or credit risk transfer, or the direction of commodity or real estate prices. For example, it is clear that the US automobile industry was not prepared for the recent volatility in oil prices. The 'Big Three' US manufacturers were largely working on a view that oil would remain inexpensive to US consumers. Meanwhile, the likes of Toyota and Honda were making calculated investments in hybrid cars and other high-efficiency vehicles to position themselves for an upswing in oil prices. In many ways, the Japanese carmakers had already 'readied their response' to the risk posed by higher oil prices and the subsequent impact on their customers. This reflects a treatment of risk on the part of Toyota and Honda as part of their corporate strategies.

This forward thinking about risk is crucial. Neither company was immune to the recent economic downturn, nor did they completely abandon the previously lucrative American SUV market, but both were better positioned than their big US counterparts because they were better prepared. They identified a risk and took action in a way that would allow their corporate strategy to adapt to an environment with lower consumer interest in large vehicles.

The emphasis is on 'readying the response', in much the same way that armies conduct simulations to prepare for a yet-unseen conflict. Companies that ready a response for a range of situations are not necessarily better at predicting the future; they are just more prepared for what comes to pass. This continuous preparation often makes them better at understanding factors predictive of a risk. So, being ready is not preparing for doomsday, but rather being able and prepared to adapt.

The phrase 'liquidity risk' has been used to describe the woes of many companies. In fact, it is a more polite way of saying that an organisation has run out of money. The seeds of today's liquidity risks were sewn a few years ago, during more prosperous times, when companies dispersed excess cash through dividends and share buy-backs, and undertook a wave of high-priced mergers. Indeed, shareholders clamoured for this sharing of wealth and punished those companies that held 'excessive cash reserves.' However, today those organisations that hoarded cash can better protect themselves against 'liquidity risk' and can purchase competitor assets at significant discounts.

Warren Buffett's Berkshire Hathaway is a good example of this. Its policy of not paying a dividend drew naysayers in the past, but it means that the company now has cash when it is most needed. It has allowed Mr Buffett to follow a strategy of long-term value for investors. The implicit risk decision was tied to strategy.

> **The emphasis is on 'readying the response', in the same way that armies conduct simulations of yet-unseen wars**

The current economic situation has altered many assumptions about business and markets, and we have seen a massive investment by governments in corporations. This will surely bring new risks to both corporations and governments alike, which have different strategies and goals. Although we can more or less agree that corporations are driven to return profits to investors, the role of governments as major shareholders in banks, mortgage-holding companies, automakers and insurance companies is less clear. In part, the governments of the world have provided rescue plans aimed at stabilising markets. But such investments come with a price tag. We have already seen US Congress and the UK parliament adjust and limit banks' pricing on credit cards. Banks in both countries are also restricted in taking action on defaulting mortgages, as a condition of accepting the government funds. So, the accepted risks change as the corporate strategy changes. Governments and politicians are more sensitive to public outcries than corporations, suggesting that companies accepting state assistance will likely face a new list of risks and responding to a growing group of constituents. The risk of regulation is high for many industries, and companies should adjust their corporate strategies accordingly.

In driving corporate strategy, risk management involves much more than just a set of best practices and the transferring of risk. It involves clear identification of the risks accepted. Factors that are believed to drive risk and the data that are predictive of risk should be openly communicated, but this is not limited to a company's internal risks. As the economist Frank Knight said in 1921: 'Profit is reward for taking risk.' Companies should not only be selective in which risks they take, but also be willing to pounce when the opportunity presents itself. This involves tracking the risk position of competitors in order to understand competitive advantages.

Risk management is not an exercise in paranoia, but rather an approach to understanding uncertainty, exposures, opportunities and limits in order to make educated investments. It requires executive involvement, an emphasis on making data-driven decisions, open communication and the discipline to think through scenarios and ready responses. A great many of the winners coming out of the current economic crisis will be those that not only held a bit more cash, but had a bit more information than their competitors and were able to seize a window of opportunity.

These lessons show that risk management is really about the identification of key information and its use in the decision-making process. It is not about guidelines or the execution of conventional mathematical models. Preparing for the unknown requires having the best information, not the industry accepted 'best practice'. The risk management team belongs on the corporate strategy team, not on the phone with insurance brokers.

How to talk your way through a downturn

Whether or not your company is directly hit by a crisis, it is imperative to send out the right message to internal and external stakeholders.
By **Paul A. Argenti**

D istress has presented itself in spades in the past year with an extraordinary crisis rocking global capital markets. Stocks are fluctuating wildly and investors have watched life savings evaporate, crippling people's trust in financial institutions and, in many cases, big business as a whole.

While public scepticism and negative emotions have run high, such a time of crisis has also meant that, unlike during times of calm, companies have had an eager audience that is willing to absorb corporate messages. While filled with doubt, people have yearned to be spoken to and reassured.

During times of crisis, many companies flail by failing to act or by taking the wrong kind of action when communicating with distressed stakeholders. But in these circumstances, a crisp and transparent communication strategy can set a company apart from the competition by fortifying employee relationships, showcasing superior client/customer focus, and strengthening a company's reputation for transparency, reliability and integrity with members of the wider public. By acting quickly and communicating thoughtfully, a company can build reputational capital and weather the storm to come out on the other side perceived as a long-term leader. Below are some suggestions.

During times of economic downturn, all organisations should be aware that they are vulnerable, regardless of how much or how little they are directly implicated in the predicament. Reputation by association can all too easily cause companies in the right to be lumped in with the perpetrators who are wrong. Public fear – compounded by persistent media coverage – can further chip away at trust in a business sector, or even big business as a whole.

Beware of guilt by association

Reputational risks have intensified during the past year, with the credit crisis yielding real-life villains such as Bernard Madoff, the New York money manager and former Nasdaq chairman whose alleged $50bn fraud served as the *pièce de résistance* in the shattering of trust in financial institutions in the US. Or B. Ramalinga Raju, founder and former chairman of Satyam Computer Services, the Indian outsourcing company, who resigned after admitting he had manipulated the company's books for many years including the creation of a fictitious cash balance worth more than $1bn.

Poor communication strategies or tactics make organisations or individuals likelier targets, even if they are well-meaning and innocent. Hank Paulson, former US Treasury secretary, serves as a prime example of how not to communicate during a downturn. In recent months, his missteps turned him into a household name. Never a spin-doctor, Mr Paulson forgot that the communication of his economic recovery plan would be just as important as its actual substance. Crucially, he did not effectively market his Troubled Assets Relief Plan (Tarp) as a rescue instead of a bailout. Instead, his ineffective and soft-spined communications allowed the media to grab the reins and position the Treasury's efforts as a highly questionable $700bn bail-out of greedy banks. Making matters worse, in interviews and public communications Mr Paulson switched gears a number of times, signalling indecisiveness and even helplessness in the face of the financial storm.

Communicate early, often and clearly

Being aware of a corporation's vulnerability during a downturn is only the first step. The second, perhaps most critical step is to place more emphasis than ever on communicating clearly and consistently in such a precarious environment. During downturns, cutting communications teams as a non-revenue-generating area of an organisation may seem like an easy way to slash budgets but companies do so at their own peril. During a crisis, shareholders instinctively grasp for any shred of knowledge to hang on to and often misinterpret information. Stakeholders can end up feeling abandoned, confused or distrustful, and this can do long-term damage to a company's reputation.

Companies must also be sure to focus on employees, who, all too often, are the last to receive information. As the first point of contact for many external stakeholders, employees should be well informed and, therefore, able to project an air of confidence and stability to angst-ridden consumers and investors.

Communication crib sheet for times of crisis

During a crisis, companies can uncover opportunity by adhering to a few simple guidelines when communicating with investors, employees, the press and the general public.

- **Do not hide:** not hearing from you will breed additional suspicion and mistrust among stakeholders
- **Gather relevant information and stick to your story:** be as informed as possible to reassure stakeholders that you are in control and in the know. Switching gears or waffling signals insecurity
- **Communicate early and often:** both internally and externally. Keeping employees well informed is a vital step to keeping your organisation on message with all stakeholders
- **Centralise communications:** sending conflicting messages from different areas of a company signals disorganisation and undermines stakeholder confidence
- **Get inside the media's head:** anticipate how the press might spin first-hand or second-hand information
- **Choose communication channels thoughtfully:** how and where you say something is as crucial as what you are saying. During a period of distress, scrutiny of corporate communications is higher than ever as stakeholders clamour for information
- **Communicate directly with affected constituencies:** during times of instability and uncertainty, people want to be reassured by hearing information straight from the horse's mouth
- **Keep the business running:** even in the face of upheaval, remind stakeholders that you have not taken your eye off your primary purpose as a for-profit corporation that drives returns for investors
- **Keep values and character centre-stage:** in a period of crisis, maintaining trust is paramount. Adhering to corporate values, and using them as a navigational compass to guide corporate strategy and communications, will demonstrate stability and reliability, assuring stakeholders your head and heart are in the right place.

Figure 10.1

In the wake of the credit crisis, Bank of America enhanced its intranet site with news flash features to keep employees up to date with the stories relating to the bank that consumers were reading. The company also supplied employees with communication tools such as talking points, enabling them to more effectively address potential customer concerns over news items and the highly volatile financial services landscape.

Employee anxiety, unrest or mistrust can permeate beyond company walls to be picked up by the public. In November 2008, when Citigroup's share price plummeted to close to $3, from about $33 a year earlier, over concerns about its financial health, the bank struggled with employee leaks, allegations of in-fighting among its board of directors and a spin-off of Smith Barney, its brokerage arm. On a call to employees, Vikram Pandit, Citigroup chief executive, insisted that the company's capital position remained strong while 'rumour mongering [was] at the heart of [the] problems.'

Learn to say sorry

Candid corporate communication means publicly recognising any missteps, as well as relating lessons learnt that will help to deliver future improvements once storms have been weathered. Failure to do so during and following a period of crisis can make a company seem complacent or, worse, arrogant. Consider the opening remarks made by Jeffrey Immelt, chairman and chief executive of General Electric, during the company's annual investor outlook call in December 2008. Mr Immelt diplomatically underscored the lessons learnt during a year of earnings disappointments: 'So, we come through this I'd say having learned a lot, having navigated through some really challenging times. And, like anything else, we use it as a learning experience to get better.'

❝ Employee anxiety, unrest or mistrust can permeate beyond company walls to be picked up by the public ❞

Contrast this with another Citigroup communications oversight: in an interview with US broadcaster Charlie Rose, Mr Pandit positioned Citi as far-removed from the root of crisis, failing to acknowledge past missteps or assume responsibility for risk management failings and the resulting investor losses. 'I can completely understand how people on Main Street, people who are not close to this industry would be furious at what's happened and furious at kind of where we've gotten to...' he said. 'If you start throwing everybody under the bus, we're going to need a very large bus. Given what we have gone through, the most important thing is who can do the job going forward.'

While presenting a forward-moving plan is indeed critical, preserving goodwill with stakeholders can only happen if organisations are open and honest about their own role in and responsibility for a crisis, however small or indirect.

Use the Web 2.0 opportunity

As discussed earlier, a crisis can be an opportunity to demonstrate to your stakeholders just how strong you are as an organisation. Social media and digital communications create unlimited possibilities for corporations to have candid and personal conversations with their stakeholders. From internal and corporate blogs to websites complete with videos from management and tools such as Twitter, this is the first time that social media have played a big role in the dissemination of information during a crisis. Companies such as IBM, Dell and Ford, which faces widespread negative perceptions about itself and US automakers in general, are seizing the Web 2.0 opportunity to re-establish relationships with their stakeholders and to set the standard for transparency.

Ford's chief blogger and community manager, Scott Monty has done a great job of positioning the ailing automobile company for future success through Twitter pages, multiple posts and interviews, and a general level of savvy about Web 2.0 that most companies have not yet acquired. However, as Mr Monty said in a recent interview: 'The tools don't matter a fig. They'll change, ebb, flow and go away. But you have to approach social media from a holistic viewpoint: how is this going to touch and affect what I'm doing across the board, and what do we want to accomplish?' In other words, don't forget that goal-setting is part of strategy.

Continuity, not re-invention

While invigorating a corporate communication game plan is critical during times of distress, be aware that radical new tacks in communication strategies can breed unwanted suspicion.

In the past year, investors have been severely burnt by false promises from senior executives, most notably from Lehman Brothers, which is under US federal investigation for potentially misleading comments to investors concerning the company's financial health by Richard Fuld, former chief executive. Investors have paid the price through depleted 401k retirement saving plans and mistrust of corporate communications has increased. As a result, sudden and unexpected communications – even those with the best of intentions – can heighten public fears.

Consider GE's shares slumping 10 per cent on December 1, when the company announced an unscheduled update. The announcement turned out to be positive – reiterating the company's strong credit rating and dividend commitment – but this example demonstrates how actions perceived as 'unusual' can provoke harmful knee-jerk reactions from jittery investors, even when a company communicates well.

Increasing communication is essential, but developing a coherent communication strategy and selecting channels, timing and messages thoughtfully will be most important to avoid giving off alarmist signals. Similarly, maintaining a distinct sense of identity and focusing on corporate values becomes more essential in turbulent periods to reiterate corporate consistency and a willingness to stay focused on stakeholders' best interests.

Communication is crucial to financial risk management

The current crisis underscores how vital communication is to a company's financial risk management strategy. For a corporation to attract and retain investors, it must convey its financial and organisational picture in a clear, cohesive and trustworthy manner. Failing to do so can easily dent a financial reputation, particularly during times of crisis, when investors and consumers demand more – and even more timely – information, including why the crisis happened, how they will be affected, and what will be done to rectify the situation.

When the going gets tough, a corporation has an opportunity to showcase its mettle and position itself as an entity to be trusted through thick and thin. Such trust is built over the long term, through thoughtful words backed by action to build an authentic corporate character that stakeholders can genuinely believe in.

As J.P. Morgan, the famous industrialist, rightly explained in 1912: 'The first thing is character... before money or anything else. Money cannot buy it... because a man I do not trust could not get money from me on all the bonds in Christendom.'

Getting staff on your side

During a downturn, listening to employees and setting realistic goals helps to maintain trust and dedication. By **Michael Gibbs**

These are tough times. Most industries are in recession; many companies are at risk of failing. Fear of lay-offs pervades the workplace as negative economic news accumulates and it can be difficult to motivate staff – but this is when you need them most.

In tough times, the best managers stand out even more. Moreover, handling staff well now can pay high dividends when good times return. My research and experience suggests ways to make incentive systems work effectively even in this economic climate. Below are some suggestions of how to think through goal setting and evaluation.

What to emphasise?

Every incentive plan evaluates employee performance in some way, and most make use of goals as thresholds for earning rewards or to set expectations for performance. The business climate has changed dramatically, and there are different pressures on business now, so goals and evaluation may need to change. What should be emphasised?

Usually, incentive plans are criticised for being too short-term oriented. That is because they tend to focus on things that are easy to measure, whereas the effect an employee's performance has on the future is difficult to quantify.

In today's environment, however, a short-term orientation is often appropriate. Given the weak credit market, many companies need to manage for cash, and are concerned about the inability of customers to pay receivables. Incentives for better management of receivables, cost cutting, or temporary reductions in areas of discretionary spending, can be a good idea. However, implementation must be carefully monitored, as overly aggressive incentives to manage for cash can lead employees to manipulate numbers, damage relationships with clients, defer essential maintenance, and so on.

In this economy, most managers are compelled to give less emphasis to strategy and more to tactics. Doing so means tapping into the creativity and initiative of employees, who often have many ideas about ways to improve operations and cut costs. To motivate this creativity, you must give broader discretion to staff over methods. Focus on broadly stated goals ('cut costs ' or 'increase revenue '). Then measure outcomes instead of specific inputs (total revenue instead of number of new customers). This gives your employees latitude to try different methods and see what works best to achieve your objectives.

Determining the right level of expected performance is never easy, but it is even more difficult in 2009. There is great volatility and uncertainty about the future, and performance in recent years is less likely to be a good indicator than in more stable years. Even if you can be relatively confident about expected performance, the highly volatile economy means that actual performance may well overshoot or undershoot expectations by a wide margin. If the employee finds the goal too easy or too difficult to achieve, poor motivation may result. How can you set goals in such an environment?

Set meaningful goals

Consider using shorter time horizons. Instead of stating goals for the entire year, set goals on a quarterly basis. Predictions over a shorter horizon are more likely to be accurate. An additional benefit is that your staff have a better idea of where they stand and what level of compensation they can expect. The tie between their actions and their rewards is stronger. Finally, a shorter horizon allows you to change expectations or criteria more quickly as the economic situation unfolds.

In highly volatile times, it makes sense to set easier-to-achieve goals than during more stable times. Goals may not be met because the employee was ineffective, or because of events beyond their control. It does not make sense to punish employees for factors beyond their control, especially when they are already nervous about their jobs and compensation. In the current downturn, there is greater risk that uncontrollable events will result in poor performance. It is appropriate to take some of this risk of failure away from employees by recognising that such risk is beyond their control.

Many companies use growth-based targets or performance measures. For example, a salesman might be rewarded based on the percentage increase in sales compared with last year. This approach has some downsides, but provides automatic goal setting. Growth-based targets may make sense when last year's performance is easily replicated this year compared with bringing in new business. However, they are problematic when the economy slows rapidly. This year it will be difficult to increase performance compared with last year; in fact, the economic performance of many companies will be negative. Great care must be used in implementing growth-based incentives. If your company uses them, give serious thought to eliminating the practice in the short-term.

In a year when it is hard to know what performance is reasonable to expect, one tool that may help is benchmarking: holding employees accountable for performance relative to some comparison group. Individual salespeople could be evaluated compared with average sales (or average growth) across all salespeople. A chief executive could be evaluated on the company's earnings per share compared with competitors in the same industry. Even in a volatile year, as long as the volatility has a similar effect on the employee and the comparison group, benchmarking can improve the accuracy of evaluation.

However, access to a good comparison group is critical. If the group the employee is measured against is not working in similar circumstances, benchmarking will only add more error to the evaluation. Consider our example of a specific salesperson measured against other salespeople. If sales territories vary widely in size, type of customer, economic conditions or other factors, benchmarking will hold the salesperson to a standard that does not reflect his or her job.

Finally, an important part of virtually any incentive plan is good judgment, especially in 2009. There is simply too much complexity and uncertainty to expect that even the best-designed incentive plan will fit the circumstances adequately. Good judgment can have multiple benefits. Consider using subjectively determined goals and performance evaluation rather than reliance only on numbers. Business conditions are changing rapidly. You may need to reassign people to different jobs, or reallocate tasks.

What you think will be important may turn out to be irrelevant; unexpected situations are likely to arise. Stating qualitative goals and expectations about performance may work better than tying rewards to explicit performance metrics. This gives you the flexibility to adapt those goals over time, much like the effect of using shorter time horizons, and to incorporate input from staff.

Also, reserve the right to change the incentive system at any time. You may not need to, but by making clear that you might, less conflict will arise if you do. If you use careful judgment, and establish trust with your employees, adapting poorly designed incentives will be preferable to leaving the system unaltered.

Collaborate

Economists, psychologists and human resource practitioners tend to agree that the job characteristic that employees value most is feeling that they can trust their supervisor. In tough times, with companies implementing lay-offs, it is even more of an issue.

What can you do to improve trust? Broadly speaking, collaborate with your employees on goal setting and evaluation, and in addressing the problems that your business faces. Sit down with each employee, discuss the current situation, and describe the kind of behaviour you are looking for (such as the creativity and initiative mentioned above). Using their input in goal setting and evaluation makes goals more realistic and relevant, and reduces employee risk. It provides buy-in and builds trust. Meet regularly to re-assess goals as the situation evolves. Of course, this is simply Peter Drucker's 'Management by Objectives ' approach. That method is often very effective but is particularly well suited to volatile times such as these.

Regular discussion about subjective goals has an additional advantage: manipulation is more likely when the economy is weak and employees are under high pressure. A collaborative approach to evaluation and monitoring makes it easier to detect, and thus deter, manipulation. In addition, manipulation tends to be easier when performance is based on pre-set metrics rather than retrospective judgment.

Communicate and listen. Be open about the challenges facing the business. In many cases, providing real-time data on the company's economic situation will be helpful. The environment is already risky enough, so listening and responding to employee feedback about the incentive system is important. If your employees believe that you are trying to treat them fairly and provide the tools they need to succeed, they are more likely to respond by working hard and creatively to improve the company's prospects.

Rise to the occasion

Managers face great challenges in 2009. But this is also an excellent time to improve your abilities as a leader. Self-reflection and continuous improvement in your management style now will make you a better manager for the rest of your career. In addition, by asking your staff to help you address a difficult economic situation, and then carefully listening and incorporating their concerns and ideas, you will increase your reputation as a manager who is trusted and good to work for. That is an excellent foundation for growth when the recession inevitably ends.

12

Optimists have a bright future

Leaders who see opportunity where others see gloom, and maintain focus and integrity, will win out. By **Peter Lorange**

There is much doomsday talk amid the global economic slowdown but managers should look at turbulent times for what they are: opportunities. There needs to be a fundamental change of mindset in how business leaders approach tumultuous times. Semantics do matter, so let's begin by eliminating the term 'crisis management' and replace it with 'unexpected opportunity management'.

Leading in turbulent times requires optimism. The world is constantly changing during good and bad economic times and managers need to have an appetite for rapid change. Managers who lack that mindset should be doing something other than leading a business unit within an organisation.

Both good and bad economic times are short-lived, but many leaders fail to understand business cycles. Markets always swing, so being comfortable with 'in/out', 'long/short' and 'turning point' decisions is essential to leadership. It is important to keep in mind, particularly during a downturn, that markets will always come back. It is when the markets are down that undervalued assets can, and should, be picked up. To 'play on the market movements' requires high focus on free cash flows – particularly critical in turbulent times.

Stay positive

Numerous investors made their fortunes by strategically investing during a downturn. Warren Buffett once famously said: 'Be fearful when others are greedy and greedy only when others are fearful.' This attitude requires a positive mindset.

A leader must never talk about damages, but should instead focus on opportunities. A realistic, but optimistic, approach will be far more beneficial for an organisation than one that is realistic and pessimistic. Anxiety and fear do not move an organisation forward when the going gets tough. Risks need to be looked at with optimism.

Perhaps no one exemplifies this better than Carlos Ghosn. He joined Nissan in 1999 as chief operating officer, became president in 2000 and was named chief executive a year later. At the time, Nissan was in dire straits, with ballooning debt and financial losses. While many were convinced of the company's ultimate demise, Mr Ghosn was so confident that his business strategy would succeed that he vowed to resign if certain objectives were not met within a determined time frame. This approach was so successful that it helped lead Nissan to improbable profitability.

Think pragmatically

No manager can predict future economic conditions with 100 per cent accuracy, but a smart leader can prepare his or her team for difficult times ahead. The number one way they can do this is by ensuring that the team is able to think pragmatically. If this is in place, the organisation will be able to react.

" Huge pay differences between workers and top management indicate imbalances and create unnecessary friction "

This implies a shift away from extensive systematic prior analysis, testing and planning towards earlier implementation followed by subsequent adjustment. Learning through doing is a key part of this. Plans and budgets need to be much less deterministic and much less extensive. Instead, the emphasis is to get it right through 'trial and error' while avoiding analysis to paralysis.

This means understanding the relevant underlying critical success factors, effective human resource management, respecting competitive limits and focusing on a smaller set of key strategies. The result is a clear tendency towards simplifying things – to gain more in-depth focus – and thus higher speed. Leaders have to reckon more with their own cognitive limits and realise that strategy is a choice.

One might assume, for example, that Singapore Airlines was in dire straits in the late 1990s, given that much of Asia was in the grip of a major economic crisis. However, the management team at Singapore Airlines was flexible and quick in meeting the demands of the time. Consequently, the airline further established itself as one of the most profitable in the world and as one of Asia's biggest brands.

Management teams must find a meeting place – preferably away from the main office – where they can freely debate and generate new ideas. This allows managers to share competencies, implement co-ordinated change more rapidly and develop or renew strategies and/or prepare execution plans for implementation. Business schools can be effective in this capacity by focusing on 'action learning', which blends academic expertise and relevant research with practical discussions among executives, who return to work with execution plans.

During periods of stability, the tendency is to focus on serving the interests of one particular stakeholder group: the shareholders. A finance-driven focus often prevails.

One major dilemma facing business leaders during periods of extreme turbulence is how to maintain credibility with owners and investors (internal) while focusing on external stakeholders. All major stakeholder groups must back the strategy, from the employees of the organisation (including upper/top management), banks, suppliers and stockholders. Thus, management stability is essential in order to avoid friction among non-cooperating stakeholders groups.

With the recent excesses in management bonus packages based on companies' financial performance, this bias in stakeholder focus has become highlighted. Huge pay differences between workers and top management also indicate imbalances. This creates unnecessary friction. In times of crisis, stakeholders need to be aligned to avoid a finger-pointing, me-versus-you attitude. Organisations must work more than ever with labour unions to create harmony. For example, it will be difficult for the US auto bail-out to work unless the automakers, unions and government are all on the same page. Swiss Air suffered because of its inability to collaborate in an effective manner with the Pilots Union.

Last but not least, leaders must demonstrate integrity in their actions. They must maintain trust while offering direction. One of the major reasons for the current financial crisis is that bankers stopped trusting each other, the inter-bank money flows dried up and default became prevalent. Consequently, trade slowed, resulting in tumbling stock markets, a reduction in manufacturing output, bankruptcies, government interventions and the cutting of interest rates.

The fact that executives have cashed in on lucrative bonuses while ordinary people have lost their homes has only worsened the image of banks. Hopefully, this will serve as a lesson that will lead to a new form of responsible leadership that focuses on getting positive results in the right way. Leaders must find the right balance between short- and long-term demands and focus on businesses that they truly understand.

The above described leadership qualities of optimism, speed, alignment and integrity are the recipe for succeeding in these turbulent times. The leaders of organisations which establish these attributes as best practice will no doubt seize opportunities and come out as the winners. A very different fate awaits the negative, slow, unaligned and irresponsible.

Rethinking links in the global supply chain

New methods of partnering for product development can help companies profit from demand shifts. By **ManMohan S. Sodhi** and **Christopher S. Tang**

When you have a real lemon on your hands, like the present economic downturn, you should think lemonade. This bitter and difficult financial crisis provides an opportunity to rethink an entire business and, more specifically, its supply chain.

This is a good time not only to look at initiatives to improve the company cash flow in the near term but also to think about long-term issues such as being in markets with zero growth. In the short term, there is a need to lower operating costs, for instance by outsourcing supply chain functions with demonstrable savings or by shedding projects whose incremental benefits cannot justify incremental costs in the near term.

The following ideas will help in meeting goals with regards to cutting costs, preparing for supply chain disruption, and improving your standing as a corporate citizen.

Combine lean and green

Lean means less waste and less waste means using fewer resources. Any company can make small improvements in its supply chain that collectively can lower costs and improve supply chain sustainability significantly.

Marks and Spencer, the UK retailer, has taken a leadership role in sustainability among its peers with its 'Plan A', which is intended to reduce energy consumption by 25 per cent for all its operations by 2012. The implementation comprises many small efforts including replacing 90-watt light bulbs with 75-watt bulbs in its food stores in the UK. This not only reduces energy consumption by 17 per cent for lighting but also reduces refrigeration and air conditioning needs.

Packaging is another area to explore. Tetley Tea developed new packaging materials to increase the density per pallet of its products by 50 per cent, thereby reducing the number of vehicle loads between factory and warehouse by 28 per cent.

Planned obsolescence can make sense in rapidly innovating industries such as consumer electronics but in the wake of the downturn, the industry may have to make products with significantly longer lives. Doing so will result in reduced use of resources and less need for recycling, a burden that is likely to fall on manufacturers themselves in the coming years.

Tie pricing to supply chains

This is important to improve margins, not only in the present economic downturn but even more so in the long term, when developed markets face the prospect of zero growth for an uncertain period of time. Airlines and hotels, for example, use dynamic pricing to their advantage for individual customers. Similarly, manufacturing companies can use dynamic pricing by customising and delivering bundles of products and services for individual customers with different prices.

“ When developing the iPod, Apple provided up-front payment to entice integrated circuit manufacturers ”

Dell, the computer manufacturer, adjusts prices dynamically to influence customers' product selection. When it faced a supply shortage of certain components from its Taiwanese suppliers after an earthquake in 1999, the company offered special price incentives to induce online customers to buy computers that utilised components from other countries.

Amazon, the online retailer, offers discounts to customers willing to reserve new products in advance. By using early sales data, Amazon can develop more accurate demand forecasts.

Companies can also rethink what they are selling. Bundling products and services enables organisations to differentiate themselves: for example, IBM's acquisition of PwC's consulting division in 2002 helped the IT group to further transform its business model from selling computing products to offering business solutions.

Companies can also develop in-house capabilities for services. Best Buy, the US electronics and home appliance retailer, moved to selling bundles of products and after-sales services provided by its 'Geek Squad Agents'. This strategy increases revenues and profits, and boosts customer satisfaction long after point-of-sale. General Electric customises its services bundle for each customer when selling turbines or medical equipment. Using such bundling, companies can implement 'value-based pricing' at the individual customer level, but doing so requires adapting the supply chain to streamline the delivery of these bundles, including services, and improving their understanding of how customers use (or re-sell) their products.

Shorten supply chains

Shortening supply chains means not only moving manufacturing or sourcing closer to existing markets but also developing markets in the low-cost countries where manufacturing or sourcing take place. Shorter supply chains mean more agility, more robustness against disruption, lower exchange rate risk and, in the long run, lower costs. While many apparel makers source from low-cost countries such as China and India, Zara, the Spanish clothing retailer, has banked on its European plants to create and respond quickly to new market trends in Europe with a design-to-shelf time of only two weeks. Having European plants means it has lower transportation costs to its markets in Europe.

In Japan, some electronics manufacturers have moved core manufacturing back to high-cost Japan, giving them greater agility in responding to demand as well as better intellectual property protection. Sourcing closer to home can also help companies to gain recognition as good corporate citizens.

Today's low-cost sources are tomorrow's markets and western companies with a well-established global brand image can demand a price premium. For example, Shanghai GM, a joint venture between General Motors and the Shanghai Automotive Industry Corporation, produces and sells Buicks in China at a premium despite having lower costs of production than in other markets.

Selling in China and India means having different types of supply chains for different market segments. The best example is Hindustan Unilever Limited (HUL), the largest fast-moving-consumer-goods company in India. The company's brands span the affordability spectrum, from top-end cosmetics to low-priced shampoo sachets. The HUL supply chain has adapted itself to meet customised requirements at the top end while driving cost-focused efficiencies to deliver and sell several billion sachets a year.

Reassess outsourcing and external partnerships

Companies are becoming more open to ideas and solutions from external parties. Procter and Gamble's so-called 'Connect + Develop' business innovation model, which was launched in 2002, reduces the time and cost of product development by reaching out to other companies and academia for ideas for new products. For example, when P&G wanted to print text and images on Pringles potato crisps, it partnered with an Italian professor who had developed the relevant technology. This approach to innovation has enabled P&G to achieve phenomenal double-digit growth in sales and profit over the period since 2003.

In China, Hong Kong-based trading company Li and Fung provides supply chain management services to customers such as Kohl's, the US department store chain. Li and Fung uses its network of more than 6,000 suppliers across Asia to provide services ranging from design, sourcing, supply management, and quality inspection to logistics for its global customers.

However, outsourcing and partnerships require simple and transparent ways to share the pain and the gain. For example, when developing the iPod, Apple provided up-front payment to share the development costs of specialised chips in order to entice integrated circuit manufacturers such as Samsung and Micron. Toyota also provided similar incentives for Matsushita to develop the battery for the Prius hybrid car.

Conclusion

Cost-cutting can only go so far. Companies also need to seek additional revenues and higher profit margins. Being lean and green can generate additional profits in the long term. Just as Tetley's trucks now carry loads for their customers rather than coming back empty, there may be revenue opportunities in cost-reduction initiatives as consumers become more willing to pay a premium for eco-friendly products. Shorter supply chains and new methods of partnering for product development will make companies better positioned to take advantage of changing demand. Dynamic pricing means higher average prices – this is especially important when revenues are not growing – but companies must better understand what generates value for their customers.

The present downturn poses a long list of uncertainties in the year ahead. Nevertheless, if you squeeze the downturn lemon right, you should be able to enjoy lemonade for a long time to come.

Looking long term on the passage to 'Chindia'

How can companies leverage operations in China and India during the downturn? By **Jayashankar M. Swaminathan**

Numerous companies such as Google, Microsoft, Toyota, Sony and Nokia have benefited from global operations during the past decade. A central component of this success has been the expansion of their supply chains into a number of emerging economies, particularly China and India. These countries serve as inexpensive bases for the production of goods and services on the supply side and have also become important markets for finished products on the demand side.

When the current downturn began, it was tempting to believe that the rapid growth of their internal markets would insulate China and India. The realisation is rapidly dawning, however, that in a highly interconnected business and financial world no country will be completely immune. Most recently, China has reported a growth rate of 6.8 per cent for the fourth quarter of 2008 while India has predicted a growth rate of 7 per cent for 2009. Both these figures are much lower than the growth in previous years.

Multinationals are beginning to rethink their 'Chindia' strategy and many are contemplating a range of defensive actions. These include planning for a temporary shutdown of facilities in these countries to match supply and demand, or even contemplating an early exit from them. Such reactions may provide quick short-term solutions. For long-term success, however, a more nuanced response is required. Here are five suggestions that can help companies design a strategy.

Focus on the sector, not the economy

The impact of the downturn in China and India will vary sharply across the economic sphere. Businesses in the manufacturing and consumer products sectors are likely to be significantly affected as consumers become cautious in their spending, but companies involved in infrastructural development are less likely to be affected.

National and local governments in China and India are aware of the bottleneck that poor infrastructure places on growth. This infrastructure gap in particularly acute in India. In addition, spending on infrastructure provides the government with an appealing means of economic growth going. It is no surprise, for example, that for 2009 Lafarge, a world leader in building materials, has projected growth in China and India.

Reassess offshoring

For many businesses, offshoring has become an end in itself during the past decade, leading to the notion that anything that can be offshored, must be. As unemployment rises in developed economies, companies will be under growing pressure to reassess their offshoring practices and to keep more jobs at home. This pressure might be a blessing in disguise because it provides businesses with an opportunity to critically re-examine the type and degree of offshoring they pursue.

Companies must use this opportunity to carefully consider the short-, medium- and long-term implications of offshoring. They must also evaluate whether any of their offshoring initiatives have diluted their core competencies or hampered their ability to build and leverage intellectual capital. This is a good time to adjust the boundary between the activities that the company outsources and those that it does itself.

At the least, companies should consider renegotiating their offshoring contracts with service providers in China and India who are now less busy than in the recent past. In addition, strong local companies in China and India that do not have the resources to survive the downturn may provide interesting acquisition opportunities for multinationals with cash.

Prepare for supply chain risks

After years of heady growth, providers in China and India are witnessing a sharp slowdown. For the outsourcing industry, this is the time that the wheat will be separated from the chaff. While we may only be at the leading edge of the downturn, Satyam Computers, a major India-based software services provider, has already been in the news for financial misstatements and other irregularities.

❝❝ Companies should renegotiate offshoring contracts with service providers who are now less busy ❞❞

As business slows down for some of these providers, there are greater chances that they may violate global compliance rules, which could lead to complications such as contamination (in manufacturing) and security risks (in services). It is important that multinationals pay more attention to protect themselves from such global supply chain risks during this downturn.

Improve the workforce

For multinationals who have captive operations in China and India, the downturn presents an opportunity for improving the quality of the workforce. During the past decade, many multinationals who initiated operations in these countries quickly realised that productive employees were difficult to attract and retain. This is a good time to take advantage of the weaker labour market to recruit and retain top-notch managerial talent. After all, an important benefit of running an operation in these countries is the opportunity to tap into their large pool of brainpower.

Innovate from China and India

The economic downturn will slow the rapid transition of the masses into the middle and upper middle classes in China and India. Correspondingly, the demand for high-end products and services will not grow as fast as projected. This shrinkage of the market is a challenge on the one hand, but it also offers companies the opportunity to accelerate development of affordable and robust products, designed for emerging markets. More importantly, such products could be attractive for customer segments in developed economies as well.

WITHDRAWN

SAID BUSINESS SCHOOL
EXECUTIVE
EDUCATION
LIBRARY

three

Looking beyond the crisis

Keeping a keen eye on consumer behaviour

Marketers must respond to the radical change in consumers' priorities but also ready themselves for recovery. By **John A. Quelch** and **Katherine E. Jocz**

What promises to be the longest and deepest global recession since the 1930s took many marketers by surprise. What appeared first as a crisis affecting the US home mortgage market soon morphed into a global financial meltdown and the evaporation of consumer credit.

Given an average household debt in the US of 130 per cent of annual household income, it was inevitable that a downturn in consumer confidence would follow, along with a substantial reduction in consumer spending, which accounts for 72 per cent of US gross domestic product. How should marketers, few of whom are experts in macroeconomics, respond to these conditions?

It is important to understand how customers are reacting to the new reality, how their attitudes and behaviours are changing, how easy it is for them to switch suppliers or stop buying your products and services, and whether the shifts that are evident today are going to continue once the economic recovery kicks in.

What is certain is that the market segmentation scheme you were using to plan your marketing budget and programmes this time last year is obsolete. You need to listen to your customers and possibly develop a new segmentation approach. We have identified six segments of consumers based on their response patterns to the current crisis.

We have found that the consumer mix varies across categories and across brands within categories, with stronger, trusted brands being less vulnerable to downward pressure on prices and margins:

- **Naysayers** are frightened consumers who have stopped buying any discretionary purchases and are trimming their daily purchases. They are, for example, trading down from fresh to frozen vegetables, sharing a single tube of toothpaste among family members and switching from single-purpose, specialised cosmetics to multipurpose products. They are either out of work, in fear of being laid off or know people who have been.

- **Short termers** are younger, urban consumers with few savings who have, therefore, lost little in the financial meltdown. They will carry on as normal unless and until they lose their jobs. They will then have to adjust their consumption behaviour almost overnight, as they have no savings cushion.

- **Long termers** are consumers who see the reduction in their retirement accounts as an unfortunate bump in the road. They are worried but not panicked. They are adjusting their purchasing behaviour by searching out the best deals, emphasising functional over emotional benefits, trading down to simpler versions of products they need, making fewer impulse purchases and foregoing some luxuries. However, they remain broadly optimistic and are not shutting down their consumption.

- **Simplifiers** are baby boomers who have lost a significant percentage of their savings, and, as a result, have become more risk averse and are reassessing their values. Some will conclude that they must postpone retirement to recover their net worth. Others will decide that they can make do with less, reduce their consumption and simplify their lives.

- **Sympathisers** are savvy consumers who switched into cash ahead of the crash but who know others who did not. They could afford to buy a new car but they do not want to appear ostentatious. They are continuing to spend at near-normal levels but more discreetly.

- **Permabulls** are relentlessly optimistic. Their 'here today, gone tomorrow' attitude has them looking for opportunities to make up for lost ground and find the next million dollar idea or stock pick. Their appetite for consumption remains constrained only by the availability of credit.

Marketers must understand how these six segments overlay their existing customer mix. They must understand the shifting price sensitivity of their current and potential customers and how it is affecting where and how often they shop. They must adjust accordingly the mix of marketing devoted to brand franchise building versus short-term promotions, such as coupons and rebates, that can sell products quickly, albeit at lower margins. In this recession, for example, the BMW 5 series may gain relative share at the expense of the pricier 7 series. Sports car sales may decline but demand for hybrid vehicles may hold up better than the rest of the car market.

Hope and change

Marketers must not be glum. They must balance an empathy for the financially distressed consumer with a resilient, perhaps even defiant, spirit of hope and optimism. The appropriate blend varies from one product category to another.

In general, consumers in a recession will screen out advertising messages that are based on fear appeals. There is enough uncertainty in the environment already. More appropriate are advertisements that emphasise the reasons, especially the functional features, to trust in a brand, evidence that a brand delivers value, and an emphasis on core benefits that relate to family values, friendships and relationships. Gillette's ads for its top-of-the-line Fusion shaving system justified the premium price by stressing its high-tech features, comparing the product's performance to Nascar race cars.

In the face of doom and gloom, we all need to be uplifted. Many brands in the US, for example, are attempting to piggyback on the enthusiasm for Barack Obama, US president. Ikea has called on consumers to change their furniture to mark the new president in the White House. Pepsi launched a new logo and ushered in 2009 with a celebration of 'Optimismmm'. Under the umbrella of a new slogan 'Refresh Everything', the company's website invites consumers to submit their thoughts to 'the man who is about to refresh America'.

When consumer spending power is limited, marketers are not just competing to maintain or build share in their own stagnant or shrinking product categories. They are competing against all forms of substitutes and, in a real sense, competing against all other expenditures for their share of the consumer's wallet. Brands such as Pepsi and Coca-Cola that depend for volume on millions of consumers choosing them every day must continue to project positive messages in their advertising while ensuring that their pack sizes and retail price points are adjusted to cater for a more frugal consumer.

The best antidote to margin degradation, in good times or bad, is innovation. Some companies fear launching new products in recessions – with good reason if the product is merely a superficial line extension that adds little value. But an exciting new product that offers functional value as well as emotional appeal should not be held back. For one thing, the clutter of new products competing for consumers' attention will be less than normal. Second, if you delay until the recovery comes, you will join a backlog of new products all trying to secure shelf space at the same time. Third, delaying today's product launch may delay launches of additional products you have in the pipeline, permanently undercutting your competitive edge. Rather than delaying a new product launch, shape the value proposition to address the information and reassurance needs of today's target consumers while retaining the flexibility to tweak the positioning as necessary when economic recovery arrives.

Change or die

A recession is no time to hunker down. It is a time to question the strategic rationale for non-core assets and the fundamental assumptions of your business model. Monster.com, a recruitment website, generates almost all its revenues from job posters, not job seekers. This business model works well when times are good but not when employers are firing rather than hiring. Perhaps the model should be re-evaluated to diversify Monster's revenue streams.

More important, recessions often accelerate rather than decelerate underlying trends in consumer behaviour. Take use of the internet. With consumers spending more time at home rather than going out, internet use promises to increase. At the same time, consumers anxious about current and future job opportunities are more keen than ever to develop the networks that can help them with advice and job leads. Look for professional network sites such as LinkedIn to do well and for social networking sites such as Facebook to reach out more to professionals.

Most companies are not investing in internet advertising at a rate consistent with the percentage of time that their customers spend online. A typical US consumer might spend a quarter of his or her media time surfing the internet, but a typical US advertiser might spend only 7 per cent of the communications budget on search ads, banner ads and building brand community websites. Indeed, the major packaged goods companies, including Unilever and Procter & Gamble that do not sell their products directly to consumers online, typically spend a mere 2 per cent.

However, savvy marketers are accelerating their investment in and experimentation with digital media during the downturn. Kraft Foods, for example, is experimenting with the downloading of recipes to iPhones when consumers are shopping for groceries.

❝❝ Marketers must balance an empathy for the financially distressed consumer with a resilient, even defiant, spirit of hope ❞❞

Many brands are running contests on their websites to encourage the creation of user-generated videos that are voted on by visitors to their websites. The goal is to build enthusiasm for the brand among a loyal cadre of consumers who will become the electronic spokespeople for the brand.

Of course, the recession demands adjustments in the communications mix to enable penny-pinching marketers to stretch their marketing dollars. These include substituting 15- for 30-second television ads; using less expensive radio ads instead of television to maintain advertising frequency to target customers; reducing outdoor advertising if fewer people are driving to jobs each day and others switch to public transport. But what is most important is to understand that the trend to digital is here to stay and to embrace it.

Planning for recovery

Conventional wisdom suggests that consumers return eagerly to their old attitudes and behaviours once a recession abates. Indeed, the theory is that pent-up demand during a recession is unleashed once consumer confidence rebounds and credit becomes more readily available.

This may well be true for durable goods such as cars and home appliances, which demand ever-increasing servicing costs the longer consumers hold on to them. It is, therefore, essential that manufacturers plan ahead to have the capacity available – whether internal or outsourced – to ramp up production and dealer inventories quickly. It is also predictable that, in emerging economies, consumers who were looking forward to owning their first television set or buying their first car will still want to do so once economic circumstances permit.

What is not so clear is whether all consumers in developed economies will revert to past behaviours. If the recession is long, as appears likely, new attitudes and behaviours are more likely to become ingrained. For example, preparing meals at home rather than eating out or buying in bulk are just two behaviours born of economic necessity that may continue after the recession ends. Coping mechanisms often involve collaborations with family, friends and neighbours that become a satisfying part of daily life.

Even before the recession, there was an evident move towards lifestyle simplification among baby boomers. The notion that many of us own too much stuff, that managing this stuff is expensive and cramps our style, that we may find more pleasure in experiences than owning things, that less is more, these are questions that we are more likely to ask during an economic recession. In much the same way that life-changing events such as marriage or divorce may prompt us to reappraise our basic values and goals, so an economic shock can provoke a similar response.

In no industry will the challenge of understanding customer behaviour and market segmentation be greater than in retail financial services. Consumer trust has been severely shaken as the share prices and integrity of hitherto stalwart institutions have been undermined.

Millions of investors have seen their assets slashed. Many feel cheated. How will they respond to an economic recovery? Many will remain more cautious in their investment portfolios than they should be. A second group, probably smaller in number, will be more aggressive than they should be, feeling the need to make up lost ground.

Yet opportunities will emerge from the crisis. It was no accident that John Bogle launched Vanguard, the investment management group, and Charles Schwab founded his brokerage in the wake of the recession of the early 1970s. These companies introduced new value propositions that resonated with consumers. In the same way, new value propositions will emerge from the deficit of trust induced by the current recession. Existing companies need to watch out for the flank attack from such innovative newcomers.

Finally, in planning for recovery, every marketer must understand the leading indicators that will signal a turnround in their industry and company. The generic indicators that a recovery is under way might include: sales of home safes in which to store gold bars; it takes one week rather than two weeks to get your shoes repaired; and you can actually find a parking space at Wal-Mart.

Tasting the fruits of effective innovation

Judicious cutting of redundant R&D projects can free up funds for more deserving projects and spur more imaginative use of external partnerships for long-term innovation. By **Ranjay Gulati** and **Nitin Nohria**

Recessions bring cuts in the size of the labour force, in capital expenditures, in advertising budgets, in travel, even in the loss of coffee and donuts from our meetings. Sadly, investments in research and development and innovation, the seed-corns of our future, are not insulated from these realities either. Over the past four quarters, the total R&D expenditures of S&P 500 companies (based on the approximately 200 companies that report them quarterly) declined 13 per cent – from a total of $43.1bn in the fourth quarter of 2007 to $37.4bn in the third quarter of 2008 – with more cuts almost certain in the near future.

Companies wanting to innovate will have to do more with less. But how? The process boils down to three issues: determining the overall magnitude of cuts that need to be made; deciding which projects to cut and which to maintain; and reconsidering the locus of innovation, including whether it can be done outside the traditional boundaries of the company.

The magnitude of cuts

Some reduction in R&D investments might not necessarily hurt an organisation's innovative capacity. During good times, companies tend to become lax in choosing which R&D projects to support. In a study of large multinational corporations, we found that the relationship between innovation success and resources deployed was curvilinear.

Too few resources stymied innovation, but so did too many resources, by breeding a lack of discipline and by diminishing the incentive to bring innovation projects to fruition. As with downsizing, some degree of R&D cuts can actually be productive, but going too far risks permanently shrinking the bottom line.

Where to cut

Managers must be judicious about which innovation projects they support. The example of one big US electronics manufacturer during the 1990-92 recession is instructive. Told to trim his spending by 30 per cent, the head of R&D called a meeting of everyone involved in leading the approximately 300 R&D projects then ongoing in the company. (The exact number took more than a month to pin down.) Over the course of an entire day, he forced the group to go through a series of exercises designed to slash the R&D budget by 50 per cent, well beyond the target. The process was painful, but by the end of the day about 200 projects to be axed had been identified.

He then asked managers to identify which of the 100 projects that remained could most benefit from additional spending. About 30 projects were identified, with some of their budgets increased by as much as 100 per cent. The results were stunning. More new products were brought to market that year than ever before, and the company felt it had finished the year with an even healthier innovation pipeline than it had started with. The moral of the story: do not think just about the innovation projects you can cut. Think also of how you can free up resources to give a boost to the projects with the best pay-off.

We label this the '4-4-2 Approach' – cut four, maintain four and double-up on two – but it comes with a caveat: beware that you do not overuse the approach to privilege what organisational theorist James March calls 'exploitation'-oriented innovation – projects that can generate revenues most quickly or have the best short-term pay-off – over 'exploration'-oriented innovation with more distant pay-offs that nonetheless might be vital to the company's long-term prospects.

The key lies in the mix. In the example discussed above, the company was careful to continue to invest in both, which is why it was able to strengthen its innovation pipeline while increasing the immediate flow of what came through the pipe into the market.

In cutting R&D budgets and projects, globally distributed companies must also be careful not to privilege ideas championed by the centre – those closest to the company headquarters and the traditional seats of power – at the expense of ideas championed by those who work in the company's international locations.

> ❝ Too few resources stymied innovation, but so did too many resources, by breeding a lack of discipline ❞

Projects at the centre are often marquee initiatives that the company can benefit from across the globe, what our colleagues Chris Bartlett and Sumantra Ghoshal have called 'global-for-global innovations'. But local-for-local innovations can sometimes grow into local-for-global blockbusters. Consider, for example, the small, rugged portable electrocardiogram monitor that GE Healthcare developed in India to serve local rural markets but which ultimately found markets in many other countries. In a world where the emerging markets of today may become the most important markets of tomorrow, protecting and nurturing such local innovations through the current downturn is essential.

The locus of innovation

The current turbulent R&D environment is also leading many companies to relocate the locus of innovation beyond their own boundaries. Increasingly, companies are discovering the advantages of collaborating with a range of external entities, from suppliers to universities to customers, for novel ideas. In some instances, they rely upon these external entities to autonomously produce innovation and in others they actively collaborate with them. Procter & Gamble, for example, has famously made this strategy an enterprise-wide mantra that it loosely describes as 'connect and develop'.

The benefits of externalising innovation are obvious, ranging from cost sharing to leveraging potential economies of scale. Outsourcing innovation can allow companies to both contract and expand their own footprint at the same time. As they move to aggressively reapportion R&D, companies increasingly shrink what they might consider to be 'core' activities. At the same time, they also become adept at entering into collaborative ventures in areas that allow them to expand their domain of innovation.

This simultaneous contraction and expansion can play a key role in enabling both top-line and bottom-line growth, but there are several road-blocks to get round. The first is 'core confusion'. Some companies hesitate because they are unwilling or unable to reconceptualise what they consider to be core activities and end up clinging to more than they should under the mistaken assumption that certain domains are of necessity core.

The key distinction here is between 'core' and 'critical'. Critical tasks are things such as clinical trials which, while vital to the business, do not nec-essarily provide much advantage in the marketplace. Core tasks, on the other hand, are those that provide companies with a unique advantage in the marketplace. Elements of innovation that are critical but not core can easily be externalised in ways that ensure reliable delivery from an exter-nal entity without in any way compromising marketplace advantage.

Apple's shrinking core

Perhaps no company has shrunk its core and expanded its periphery more adeptly and to greater advantage than Apple, and no Apple product better illustrates this than the company's iPhone. In creating its first mobile phone, the company leveraged the engineering capabilities of its partners, thus allowing Apple to design and deliver innovative products in record time and in a much more cost-effective way than it could have done on its own. So, while Apple created its own operating system, it partnered with developers such as Google to preload applications such as Google Maps on to the device.

Similarly, most of the hardware in the iPhone and all of the manufactur-ing of it have been outsourced. Apple carefully guards information on its supplier partners because it views this as a key source of strategic advan-tage, but shortly after the device was launched in June 2007, iSuppli, a third party, took the handset apart and found a global representation of third-party companies.

Much of the phone's core communication capability came from German semiconductor supplier Infineon. Balda, another German group, pro-vided the display module. The touch screen itself was provided by multiple sources including Japanese groups Epson Imaging Devices, Sharp and Toshiba Matsushita Display Technology. South Korean com-pany Samsung provided the applications processor and the technology for the phone's memory. iSuppli added up the estimated cost of the entire set of inputs, and calculated that the margins for Apple were likely in excess of 50 per cent.

Apple's partnership with AT&T, the sole carrier compatible with the iPhone in the US, allowed Apple to expand its periphery while also giving its partner a significant upside, including five years of exclusivity, approximately 10 per cent of iPhone sales in AT&T stores, and a small piece of Apple's iTunes revenues. In return, Apple persuaded AT&T to spend considerable time and resources to develop a new feature called 'visual voicemail' and to streamline the in-store sign-up process.

Perhaps the most vivid example of Apple's periphery-expanding alliances has been the array of partnerships it has formed to develop applications and peripherals that are sold to customers in the growing numbers of Apple stores or via its online store.

The perils of open innovation

Despite the obvious lure of open innovation, especially in perilous budget times such as these, two issues need to be tackled to fully leverage the potential advantages this has to offer. First, skilful companies recognise that a shift towards open innovation must be balanced with a strong anchor around their customers. It is tempting in an open-innovation model to be a technology-push company where countless ideas emerging from a large partner-base are funnelled through to customers in a dizzying array of offerings.

❝ By choosing which projects to cut, protect or even expand, companies can do more with less ❞

But companies must understand how to balance this push model with a customer-driven pull model as well. They need to find ways to funnel customer insight to their partner base while at the same time allowing partners to open up new frontiers that might go beyond customer imagination.

Apple has succeeded in finding a balance between what it thinks customers want and what they might need. The company directs its partners on key input requirements while allowing them considerable freedom to develop what they consider to be desirable for customers.

As collaborative innovation moves to centre stage for companies and permeates their core, they also have to recognise the importance of developing expertise in managing their growing array of partnerships. Collaboration does not come naturally to most companies.

However, the pioneers in this movement understand the importance of building a relational capability within the company. They not only embrace a set of routines and processes to become better at identifying partners and negotiating agreements, they also embed a collaborative mindset into their culture. These shifts require concerted and systematic effort.

Conclusion

Reductions in R&D budgets may be inevitable for most companies in the present context. But if made intelligently, these cuts do not have to hurt innovation. By choosing which projects to cut, protect or even expand, companies can do more with less.

Moreover, by becoming more adept at shrinking what they consider core while leveraging partners who can help them innovate in ways that are genuinely customer-centric, companies can embrace a more open approach to innovation that may pay lasting dividends, even when the economy recovers.

Sure ways to tackle uncertainty in tough times

Company leaders must develop crisis plans and display behaviour that restores trust among stakeholders. By **Neal A. Hartman**

As the global economy slows, managers face a more uncertain business environment than they have probably ever known. Successful executives will shape the future by developing a strategic plan. Uncertainty can be seen as a threat, or it can be viewed as creating possibilities.

We do not know how governments will respond or how global financial systems will behave, but managers need to examine their company and industry and consider the overall economic trends.

Challenges in a downturn

How can companies attract and keep talented employees? How can leaders reduce the amount of uncertainty surrounding their organisation? And how do managers create a company culture that can thrive in uncertainty?

Communicating clearly, consistently and honestly is key. Consider recent developments at Apple. When photographs appeared in the press showing a much thinner Steve Jobs, investors worried. Mr Jobs, the company's chairman and CEO, issued a statement to put rumours about his health to rest and this helped ease investors' concerns. Shares in Apple fell again, however, with the news that Mr Jobs' health problems were more complex than previously thought and that he was taking leave, although he would continue to be involved with key decisions. Now Apple must work hard to alleviate the uncertainty that investors perceive.

Managers need to deal with uncertainty directly. It is important to understand that people perceive uncertainty in different ways and managers should nurture the idea among stakeholders that uncertainty brings possibilities, rather than seeing it just as a threat. Managers must also share information; it is generally assumed that the more input people have into change, the more they buy into company goals.

Managers who consistently display their values and beliefs through their behaviour have a significant impact on the culture of the organisation. If employees understand that the company leaders view uncertainty as something that offers opportunities, this will be embraced throughout the organisation.

The value of planning

Although no company can develop a strategy that addresses every uncertainty, having a crisis plan in place will help, regardless of the situation that arises. It is doubtful that before September 11 2001 any of the organisations housed in New York's World Trade Center would have considered the possibility that aircraft would be flown into the buildings. Yet those companies that had a crisis plan in place dealt more effectively with the crisis and uncertainty following the event than those that had no plan.

Managers developing a plan should begin with research, using internal resources as well as outside consultants. Managers should look broadly at ideas, borrowing from other companies where appropriate. Companies should perform scenario analyses by predicting potential uncertainties, identifying relevant risks and simulating events. A team needs to be in place to deal with the events and address stakeholders; this ensures clear and consistent messages. Plans, once devised, must be constantly reviewed and revised.

Organisations must also be flexible and have the ability to quickly and efficiently try new methods in the face of changed circumstances. Developing this organisational flexibility should be a central objective of any company.

Mastering uncertainty

Managers must also pay close attention to their own actions during uncertain times. Because many people perceive uncertainty as frightening, leaders need to display behaviour that brings about a sense of trust and credibility. Uncertainty is often a source of stress, but it is how people react to this stress that determines the kind of decision-making that occurs. Effective managers are those who develop the emotional maturity to behave rationally and confidently in stressful and uncertain situations and they must nurture this ability in their employees as well.

Managers should also build social support systems, both inside and outside the organisation. Managers who work with effective teams can share experiences and gain new insights, enabling them to deal more effectively with uncertainty and sudden change.

Because uncertainty is stressful, it is important that managers learn how to manage stress. A person's ability to deal with uncertainty is better if they exercise, maintain a healthy diet, sleep well and talk about the issues. If one considers uncertainty as a vehicle of possibilities rather than a threat to current norms, the attitude is much more positive.

Managers in the 21st century must be ready to deal with the threats uncertainty brings and to think boldly and creatively about the possibilities it offers. Organisations with managers who are able to do so will prosper for years to come.

18

Plugging in to transformation

Maintaining IT investment is even more vital for survival than it was in past downturns. By **Vasant Dhar** and **Arun Sundararajan**

The current downturn is unique because it is happening in the midst of a rapid transformation of business by information technologies. This transformation has been driven most recently by the widespread adoption of broadband and Web 2.0 technologies, mobility enabled by increasingly powerful wireless devices, technological platforms of unprecedented functionality, and the emergence of commercially viable computing clouds and software services.

These turbulent economic times present new opportunities for companies that invest wisely in information technologies, and new threats for those without a sufficiently forward-looking IT investment strategy. Opportunities arise because downturns can change consumer preferences, making people experiment with new lower-cost products or modes of consumption that were not pursued seriously during more prosperous times. Dangers arise if IT spending is conducted without careful assessment of the long-term impact. This is more likely when executive attention is devoted excessively towards short-term earnings management and cost control.

IT investment strategies

So, what is the right IT investment strategy during this economic downturn? Our academic research frames three kinds of IT-related business decisions: those that react to or cause 'industry transformation', where business models are fundamentally altered by progress in information technologies; those that increase operating efficiency or productivity through the use of IT infrastructures, enterprise systems or transactional systems that enable economies of scale or complexity; and those that lead to acquiring and leveraging various kinds of 'customer intelligence' enabled by technological systems that better connect customers to products and companies to consumers.

Viewing IT investment strategy through this lens requires varying one's recessionary reaction based on which kind of IT-related decisions one is contemplating. First, IT investments associated with pending or ongoing business model transformation should be continued or ramped up. The recession will not change the fact that the basic business models of numerous industries have been and will continue to be changed by IT over the coming years. Furthermore, such transformation persists in both good and bad times. For example, the financial brokerage industry was transformed by the widespread adoption of online consumer trading systems during the build-up to the dotcom boom of the mid to late 1990s.

In contrast, the wrenching digital transformation of the music business over the past few years was affected most critically by decisions made soon after the dotcom bust in 2000. While the roots of change were evident in the emergence of the MP3 digital music format and peer-to-peer file sharing, record labels failed to make intelligent decisions about their IT strategy, shifting market power dramatically to newer intermediaries such as Apple, which exploited emerging technology platforms and changing user preferences to become the world's largest music retailer.

In industries characterised by business model transformation during downturns, it is especially important not to focus excessively on short-term IT cost control. Downturns can accelerate the pace of transformation, making it critical to think about the opportunities and threats engendered by the combination of changing preferences and technological change.

An example is video entertainment. Increasingly, consumers of conventional television and film content are also turning to alternative forms of video entertainment that are exclusively internet-based. The recession is likely to reduce spending on cinema tickets and DVDs, prompt consumers to reassess expensive cable subscriptions and shift consumption towards lower-cost online video content.

As more consumers make this switch, it is essential that film studios and TV networks invent a viable business model, rights management strategy and delivery infrastructure that supports revenue-generating digital consumption. Withdrawing their IT investments and business model development as a cost-cutting measure could have a disastrous long-term effect on the current market leaders.

Decisions about investments in infrastructures and systems that contribute towards operating efficiency can be made more conservatively. Returns from IT infrastructure investments tend to take years rather than months to materialise. Further, they do not show up unless augmented by substantial organisational and employee behaviour re-engineering, which may be hard to implement during a period of widespread hiring freezes.

Downturns induce innovative investments

In parallel, cost reduction pressures will catalyse the transition from proprietary to shared infrastructures that tap into cloud computing platforms and software as a service. These new models of corporate computing are likely to replace self-owned IT systems for non-mission-critical processes and applications. The current downturn may provide the impetus organisations need to invest in the assessment and transition planning necessary for successful migration to these lower-cost IT infrastructures.

“ Withdrawing IT investments as a cost-cutting measure could have a disastrous effect on current market leaders ”

Decisions relating to the use of information technologies to acquire and use customer intelligence are affected in various ways by the downturn. In a recessionary economy, customer retention is critical to a company's survival.

At the same time, the internet has enabled an explosion in access to electronic data, which is becoming increasingly important to truly 'understanding' people through their data trails. User-generated content is widely prevalent as people become increasingly connected and spread information about even the most obscure of topics.

Businesses can access this data relatively cheaply, thus creating the potential for IT investments that increase customer intelligence and improve the business intimacy of consumer contact. For companies that do not currently leverage electronic customer data as an asset, now might be the time to carefully assess how this could support current and future business strategy.

This assessment needs to recognise that the basic model of customer contact and marketing is being transformed by online advertising and Web 2.0 technologies, whereby companies move away from directly influencing their customers and towards either reacting to their customers' electronic intent, or mediating the influence that consumers have on one another.

At the same time, companies are now positioned to use 'crowdsourcing' technologies to obtain more complex intelligence from their customers. The richness of this intelligence is expanding substantially through the use of interactive product design that involves frequent and active electronic consumer input; from open research and innovation through the use of development contests; and from superior forecasting and business intelligence acquisition through the use of prediction markets. As customer preferences evolve in reaction to the recession, acquiring intelligence through aggressive Web 2.0 investment strategy is critical. The simple user-generated content we have seen substitute company-generated messages is just the tip of the iceberg.

Conclusion

We are analysing a unique point in history. Previous downturns occurred during times when our IT infrastructure was primitive relative to what exists today. Information has become plentiful and relatively cheap as a torrent of content flows from users to an increasingly interactive web while people simultaneously leave richer electronic data trails of their behaviour. Against this backdrop, missing the IT investment boat could set companies back more than it has done in the past.

Decisions about these investments need to be forward-looking in a way that includes an assessment of relevance to both current and anticipated future business models. Curbing spending with a short-term focus will eventually cost more than it saves, while IT investments based on an intelligent framework could generate long-term gain.

Does your M&A add value?

With deal activity slowing to a crawl, managers must look beyond indicators and focus on delivering shareholder value. By **Laurence Capron** and **Kevin Kaiser**

The market for corporate control is facing a downturn. Thanks to tough borrowing conditions, depressed stock values and the slumping global economy, the value of merger and acquisitions transactions cancelled since the beginning of October almost equals the value of deals that have been completed, according to data compiled by Thomson Reuters. Those figures do not, however, include withdrawn deals for which values were never publicly disclosed. Notable withdrawn deals include the $147bn bid for Rio Tinto, the Anglo-Brazilian mining group, by BHP Billiton, the Australian mining giant; and the failed $48.5bn buy-out of Canada's BCE telecoms by a consortium of private equity groups. The total volume of worldwide M&A deals globally fell 29 per cent in 2008 compared with 2007, with the US (down 32 per cent) and Japan (down 45 per cent) particularly hard hit.

The reduced activity in the market of corporate control, along with the collapse of iconic companies in the advisory community (investment banks, rating agencies, commercial lenders, consultants, lawyers, accountants) could be perceived as a big blow to many companies for whom acquisitions have been the preferred growth strategy in past decades. When carefully chosen, priced and executed, M&As help companies create value by providing access to new technological or human resources, exploiting learning opportunities, meeting customers' needs, exploiting economies of scale or restructuring industry capacity.

However, the current slowdown in M&A activity, notably for large trans-actions, could provide an opportunity for companies to think more carefully about their M&A strategy and the process they have been using to buy companies. Indeed, M&As in past decades have, on average, destroyed value for the acquirer's shareholders. It is therefore timely to step back and better understand the functioning of the market for corporate control in which companies operate.

Failures in the market for corporate control

Whereas acquisitions have been touted as a value-creating tool, most companies have failed to add value through acquisitions, at least in terms of shareholder value. Beyond the oft-cited reasons (failure to deliver on synergy potential, paying too high a price and integration issues), the root cause of most failures is the incentive system that encourages managers to ask the wrong questions.

Managers should ask how a potential acquisition might improve their company's ability to meet customer needs in ways that cannot be easily matched by its competitors. They should value this using expected future cash flows to ensure that the purchase price does not exceed this future value. However, most managers ask very different questions, such as: how will this impact on our earnings per share?; how will this impact on our growth rate?; how will this help us to reach market share targets?; and how will this impact on our share price and my options pay-offs?

All targets on such indicators can be achieved by one of two methods: creating value or destroying value. The difference hinges on the expected value of the benefit realised relative to the price paid to obtain it. Whenever a manager delivers on an indicator, the question should be: 'What is the value of delivering on the target and what will I have to pay to do so?'

It is important to distinguish between the overriding objective for companies, which is value creation, and the indicators that measure how well they are delivering on this objective which include, share price, EPS, market share, growth in any given indicator, customer satisfaction, etc. Most managers pursue incentives based on these indicators. The result is that managers knowingly destroy value in the pursuit of promotions/bonuses/option scheme pay-offs.

One symptom of these incentive compensation schemes is an undue focus on company size rather than value creation, due in part to the practice of benchmarking CEO compensation across companies of similar size – bigger being better. The result is that managements are willing to overpay for acquisitions and are encouraged to do so by advisers whose primary interest is often ensuring that the transaction takes place rather than ensuring that the acquirer creates value in the process.

Misaligned incentives and the current crisis

This combination of misaligned incentives and a focus on indicators rather than value contributed to the decisions made by bankers and mortgage brokers, among others, that led to the current financial crisis.

Finance and strategy scholars have found evidence of incentives misalignment between investment banks and their clients that arise when banks put their own fees and brokerage commissions ahead of client interests. Within the M&A context, powerful incentives within M&A advisory banking – such as the advisory teams' bonus pool and the bank's desire to advance in the M&A league tables by increasing deal numbers and volumes – may conflict with the interests of shareholders.

Reliable advisers with the skills to assess and advise on the value impact of M&A opportunities will gain importance

The M&A advisory community has played a significant role in the failures in the market for corporate control. This community, from investment bankers to corporate lawyers, uses incentive systems that push for aggressive transaction execution. Certification agencies have failed to provide reliable estimation of company quality and viability. This violation of shareholder trust has seriously damaged the M&A advisory community's credibility and this is likely to impact on the role in future. We believe that reliable advisers with the skills to assess and advise on the value impact of M&A opportunities will gain in importance.

Navigating the current M&A market

In the current situation, companies will need to be resourceful and creative to navigate through frictions in the M&A market. Solutions include using internally generated cash, more aggressive use of shares as acquisition currency, delayed payment schemes or other forms of vendor financing, or even using non-equity securities as acquisition currency, which essentially turns the selling company's shareholders into lenders of acquisition debt financing. These sources will be more difficult for financial buyers to access than for strategic buyers. For this reason, private equity-led acquisitions will need to be more creative still, with recent trends towards higher equity percentages, aggressive vendor financing, and 'growth-equity' investments where the returns will be driven by growth of the acquired business rather than cheap leverage.

In every case, it will remain critical that in addition to simply tapping creative financing schemes, the acquirer provides compelling arguments for value creation. Another important skill will be persistence. There will be even fewer 'quick and easy' acquisition opportunities than in the past.

This additional pressure will further reinforce the focus on the right questions, such as how could this opportunity enhance our competitive advantage or its sustainability? It will also drive development of internal skills for better identifying, screening, valuing, negotiating, structuring and integrating the right targets at the right price. All of this will help companies to get through what will be a difficult short term, and simultaneously position them to be among the first to capture the opportunities that will arise as economies rebound.

In summary, while the crisis will impose many hurdles to financing and closing transactions in the market for corporate control, it will drive home the critical need to identify and capture value from any and all opportunities. This should strengthen the skills, internally and externally, that are required to deliver on this value-creation imperative as well as the corporate governance terms between shareholders, management and advisers. More than ever, it will be crucial for managers not to manage the short-term cash positions of their companies to ensure their survival, but also prepare for and build long-term value-creating strategies for their companies.

chapter

The time is ripe for fresh ideas

Recessions are a chance for companies to abandon outdated management practices and experiment with innovations such as virtual working and group leadership. By **Lynda Gratton**

F orget business workshops and cases studies – recessions provide real-time opportunities for executive learning as old myths are brought into question and management innovations emerge.

Historically a downturn has been a time when business models, organisational structures, labour markets and employee contracts come under immense strain. Accepted wisdoms are challenged and this break in thinking can result in the adoption of new practices and the adoption of new habits and skills. These pressures and fissures – while difficult at the time – can yield fresh ideas, engaging experiments and interesting adaptations in the long run.

This is important because while many managers are adept at innovating products and services, few have been adept at innovating the practice of management itself. As a consequence, businesses are often cluttered with increasingly outdated ways of managing: performance management processes that were invented in the 1950s; notions of leadership that go back to the command control of the second world war; and meeting protocols that have not changed for decades. At the same time, potential innovations such as virtual team technology are left unheeded.

Lessons of past recessions

To understand this better, let us look at two recessions the business world has experienced in the past 30 years. The 1981–82 recession heralded the end of the notion of a 'job for life' and marked the rise of what would eventually be called the 'free agent'. With the greater autonomy of workers came experiments in flexible working and project-based work. These nascent attitudes received further impetus as technology was able to support flexibility and enabled the move of some work from the office to the home.

The 1990–92 recession accelerated these changes while adding another important dimension: globalisation. The slashing of costs that came with this recession encouraged manufacturers and, later, service providers to move work out of the developed economies to the labour markets of the emerging economies such as India and eastern Europe. What began simply as the exodus of low-cost work to emerging markets accelerated during the following 10 years and evolved into the highly sophisticated globalisation of the talent markets in sectors such as information technology and research, resulting in the rise of what has been called the 'creative class'.

The current downturn

If recessions are times that enable accelerated change in management practices, then to make the most of this acceleration managers must identify where the fissures and tensions are likely to emerge. There are two points of tension emerging in this recession that may allow for innovation in management practices.

Wider distribution of leadership

This recession has brought into stark perspective the role of the leader. Up to this point, the dominant norm has been the 'command and control' leadership style. In this model, the organisation is viewed as a hierarchy in which decisions are escalated to the top, where a CEO makes the decisions.

But many people are now questioning the wisdom of placing so much power in the hands of so few. At the same time, insights from research in decision sciences and technological advances have shown that often the best decisions are made by an 'intelligent crowd', rather than one all-powerful individual.

This is a fissure in the norms of organisational life that could well lead to the acceleration of a more democratic and distributed decision-making process and the idea that leadership can be held by a wider group of people. The wise executive takes this as an opportunity to think more profoundly about the selection and development of leaders and the means of strategic decision making.

Senior leadership cadres have traditionally been essentially homogenous – middle-aged men with similar backgrounds. While research on innovative teams has shown that such groups are likely to be less competent in decision making than diverse teams – little change has taken place. With the dominant model under question, this is a good time to bring diversity back on to the agenda. Businesses should be looking more closely at the experiences of the Norwegian government, which passed legislation requiring that women must comprise 40 percent of boards of listed companies.

Every six months, a number of important questions about the future of the company, its markets and its technologies are posed by the senior team to the whole company with the assumption that anyone can volunteer their insight and ideas on these questions. The views of these grass-root strategists are then brought together in a series of virtual and real-time meetings in which the ideas are discussed and debated. The outcomes of this collective thinking play a crucial role in the creation of the company's strategic planning and a platform on which resource allocation decisions can be made.

Creating flexible virtual teams

" With companies freezing travel budgets, many executives will have to do more work virtually "

Past recessions have often served to accelerate the adoption of management practices and processes that already had some popularity pre-recession. The same is true of the technology and mindset that supports virtual working. Assembling teams to work on projects and task forces has become more viable in the past decade, often hastened by the pressures of globalisation. Yet while virtual working is emerging as a trend, there is still an assumption that face-to-face working trumps virtual working. At the same time, research I have conducted with my colleagues on teams across the world has shown that many fail to utilise the technologies available to them.

As a result, every Sunday night thousands of executives board aircraft and trains to get to Monday morning meetings. With many companies freezing travel budgets, this is likely to change and many executives will have to do more work virtually.

At the same time, the entry and exit roads of the world's big cities are clogged from early dawn with commuters hurrying to and from work. This movement of people has been based on two assumptions: that people need to meet every day to get their work done; and that when at home, they are likely to slack and they, therefore, need the discipline of an office to ensure they perform.

Both assumptions are wrong. First, people do not need to meet every day to get their work done. Our research has shown that virtual teams – where members rarely meet – can be highly productive. What is important in these teams is that they are all inspired by a meaningful task, fascinating question or compelling vision. So, while it is indeed important for people to establish a working relationship, we have discovered that more productive and innovative teams focus on completing a shared task rather than meeting each other face to face.

For example, the vast majority of the many thousands of volunteers across the world who every night build and repair the Linux open-source software platform have never met each other in real life. Theirs is a community built exclusively in the virtual world, powered by a compelling vision and shaped by individual commitment.

The second assumption – that people need the discipline of an office to ensure they perform – is also a myth that is well past its sell-by date. During the past decade, much research and practical examples have shown that when people have the opportunity to work on engaging, well-planned tasks at home they are significantly more productive and committed than those who toil through the commuter traffic every day.

I predict that we will see a sharp rise in the number of virtual teams that include home-based members. This will require us to abandon some old team habits and learn some new ones. It will also require us to build a much deeper understanding of which factors drive the performance of virtual teams and how these teams can be actively developed.

Opportunities in a downturn

So how can executives respond to the opportunities this recession will provide for innovation in management? It is a two-stage process. First, create space by jettisoning what is not needed, and second, begin to experiment with new practices.

What can be jettisoned? One of the worst predominant management practices has been the preponderance of face-to-face meetings. In highly skilled hands, these meetings can be a dynamic activity and a crucial decision-making platform, but too often they decay into something much less productive. Now is a good time to question the number of face-to-face meetings. And, if some of these meetings are crucial, then take a leaf out of BP's book and train even the most senior executives in facilitation and dialogue skills.

Next, consider which experiments can be conducted immediately that would enable the business to develop new and innovative management practices. Here are some candidates for challenging experimentation that can work well in a recession:

- Follow the lead of the Norwegian government and rapidly increase gender diversity at senior levels by putting in place quotas for the proportion of women short-listed and appointed in roles.
- Question the existing logic that determines how decisions are made by following Nokia's lead and experimenting with strategy formation from the bottom up – rather than always going for the top down.
- Restrict travel to encourage virtual teams. Take a closer look at how they work and experiment with ways of supporting them.
- Put group-ware technologies at the top of the performance agenda. Experiment with video conferencing, webcasts and group decision-making tools.

Not all of these experiments will flourish and some will die out over time. I would expect, for example, that while we will see more virtual teams and greater use of the technologies that support them, once cost cutting is relaxed, some people will return to airports. Others, however, will have fundamentally changed their habits and begun to build working communities that are virtual and highly productive.

Recessions are a time of destruction of the old order, a time when assumptions are questioned and nascent practices and ideas are given space to flourish. That is little cheer for now but, in the longer term, an enormous stimulus for change.

Play fair with workers to reap rich rewards

Tough decisions and cost cuts are inevitable, but if properly executed they can clarify a company's identity and purpose. By **Batia Mishan Wiesenfeld**

T he economic downturn has brought millions of lay-offs, leaving most companies populated by employees who could be best characterised as 'survivors'. As the recession continues, some companies will use this period to establish a platform on which to shape growth and success when the economy turns round. For others, declining performance will lead to wave after wave of redundancies in a seemingly inexorable downward spiral.

What differentiates the companies that will weather this downturn from the ones that will fail? The ones that succeed will be those that recognise that their lifeblood is the motivation and commitment of their remaining employees. While the traditional rewards that managers use to motivate employees, such as promotions, pay increases and bonuses are in scarce supply in difficult times, there are other steps managers can take, for free or at little cost, to strengthen morale.

The single most important thing managers can do is to plan and implement decisions in a manner that is fair – especially those related to downsizing. What do we mean by fair? Decisions are perceived as fair when they are implemented consistently and without bias, are based on thoughtful analysis rather than politics or whim, and when they are explained. Employees sense fairness when they are given advance notice of changes and an opportunity to provide input, wherever appropriate, and are treated with dignity and respect.

Fair procedures reduce the likelihood that employees who are made redundant will file a wrongful termination lawsuit. Furthermore, in years of research studying thousands of lay-off survivors across organisations and industries, my colleagues and I have found that when lay-off procedures are fair, remaining employees are more committed, more motivated, more creative, report a more positive and co-operative work group climate, and are more confident and less likely to leave the company.

For example, in one large non-profit organisation, managers role-played breaking the bad news to lay-off victims in order to prepare themselves to be sensitive, rather than formal and abrupt. An employee survey showed that morale did not decline after the lay-offs because of how the redundancies were handled. In a large bank that was previously riven by political factions and infighting, using consistent and transparent procedures to allocate jobs and cut staff after a merger actually enhanced *esprit de corps* and helped to facilitate co-ordination across units.

What do fair procedures require? One common misconception is that, in order to be fair, managers should ensure organisational survival while avoiding tough decisions or cost cuts. However, being fair is not about straying from hard choices. Fairness is not defined by the *what* that must be done, but rather *how* it is done.

Fair procedures reassure employees that they will get their share of desired outcomes in the long run and can help to convey a company's-positive character and identity. Unfair procedures, by contrast, tell employees that the organisation's values are undesirable and that employees are not valued. My research has found that employees who are treated unfairly are more likely to prioritise their own self-interest, focus on the short term, micro-manage subordinates and projects, and protect themselves through methods such as deflecting responsibility and avoiding risk.

For example, in a supermarket chain, employee theft increased significantly after a poorly managed cost-cutting initiative. In stark contrast, employees who are treated fairly are more likely to act in the organisation's interests, take a long-term view, empower and help other employees and invest themselves in their jobs and companies, such as through innovative ideas and actions.

Focus on remaining staff

While the global downturn poses a host of threats, it also provides an opportunity for savvy managers. Employees are attempting to make sense of their circumstances and to establish a new set of expectations. They are, therefore, especially open to words and signals from management that define the company's identity and purpose. Although employees may exude negativity and cynicism in difficult times, most are looking for something to believe in. Managers must, therefore, refocus employee attention on goals, missions and purpose. When employees perceive that purpose as valuable, they are more likely to accept the organisation's identity and work hard to align their goals with those of the company. When their assessment is negative, they are more likely to withdraw.

For example, in a large European public hospital, staff interpreted cost-cutting as evidence that management was willing to sacrifice patient care. This occurred because managers failed to draw a link between the cuts and the aim to remain a local hospital that could best serve the immediate community. This failure to connect managerial decisions with organisational identity led to increases in employee turnover and absenteeism.

How to make fairness clear

Clarifying what the organisation stands for requires well thought out ideas and consistent communication, but relatively few resources. It is essential that managers articulate why decisions are made and why the organisation has set particular goals.

This helps employees to see the link between their own roles and the larger whole. An added benefit is that such discussions prompt reflection, which can expose erroneous assumptions and allow them to be corrected.

Employee attention should be directed outward to combat the tendency for resource scarcity to provoke unproductive internal competition. For example, employees and departments can evaluate themselves in relation to the value they deliver to customers, rather than the return they deliver to shareholders. Serving the customer is personally rewarding and builds employees' sense of competence. Customer feedback directs employee effort without managerial intervention. To take advantage of this, managers must help staff to understand who their customers are, and the factors that shape their satisfaction.

Building organisational identity and implementing change in a fair manner requires managerial commitment, but it can be accomplished without additional expenditure. For managers forced to downsize during the downturn, this could prove to be beneficial for business growth and sustainability in the long term.

part

four

The future business environment

New thinking on how to do business

Recession will prompt radical changes in the rules and roles of sectors. How companies respond will determine their future.
By **Michael G. Jacobides**

A s the previous three issues in this series have illustrated, we are living through a unique time in several ways. Not only is this recession probably the worst since the second world war, but it also caught us by surprise.

Over the past few decades, economic theories have become increasingly sophisticated, borrowing analytical tools from theoretical physics and mathematics. Financial tools have become vastly more complex. Regulators have created sophisticated rules to govern the economy, particularly banks.

So why did we not see this coming? And how did last year's 'strong incentives' and 'profit-driven behaviour' become today's 'reckless profiteering' and 'abuse of the system'?

One reason is that we neglected basic economic facts and failed to appreciate the evolving structure of industries and sectors. In the past decade, what I term the 'industry architecture' – the rules and roles that govern how participants do business – in financial services changed the financial world dramatically, but almost nobody noticed. Most economists did not bother – for them, industry structure (in particular, the business models operating in the sector) is of secondary interest – and they stuck to the mantra that 'markets regulate themselves'. Regulators ignored the monumental changes in how money was made, concentrating instead on fine-tuning rules that focused on an ever-decreasing part of the business world. Academics busied themselves with models that had less and less to do with reality, helping to create structures so complicated that they were bound to implode. And management gurus did not want to spoil the party by suggesting that there were no solid foundations for this brave new world.

So much for the bad news. The silver lining to the cloud is that a better understanding of the industry architecture (especially in financial services) will help us to understand both the causes and the remedy for our malaise. This crisis could be a wake-up call, showing us how some companies manage industry architectures to their advantage – and how some industries are dangerously unstable. Armed with this insight, we can take advantage of the opportunities presented by this downturn to reshape companies and even sectors.

What is industry architecture and why does it matter?

Industry architectures consist of the roles played by companies in a sector and the rules (standards, regulations and conventions) that connect them. They define the ways in which money is made – companies' business models. They influence 'who does what' (strategic choices, and what each role is in the industry) – which, in turn, determines 'who takes what' (revenues, market share, competitive advantage and profit). However, they are not static – they change substantially over time.

Consider financial services. Over the past decade, we have seen new instruments (securitised loans and, later, collateralised debt obligations), new rules (often promoted by the companies and individuals who stood to benefit from them) and new models (varying types of hedge funds). These changes transformed the way money was made and created new winners: securitisers in the beginning of the decade, hedge funds and private equity shortly thereafter and (until the collapse) all their employees.

What is interesting about industry architectures is that they often change without us noticing; indeed, I only helped coined the term 'industry architecture' in 2006. Since nobody is meant to monitor them, industry architectures can lead to boom or bust – or both. If you take a step back and get a sense of the entire system, you might see the risks and opportunities. But if you do not, you might get a meltdown. Thus, each successive change in financial services was eminently sensible in isolation – but their cumulative impact was disastrous, and someone should have foreseen it.

What went wrong in financial services?

The first change was the arrival of securitisers: new players who found a novel way of slicing and dicing risk for profit. The problem was that the risk rating agencies, who were supposed to be the gatekeepers, were not up to the task. Their flawed business model, where profits were made from risk rating and costs were associated with the expertise of the executives doing the rating and the time they spent on it, practically guaranteed that supervision would deteriorate.

Then came the collateralised loan obligation/ collateralised debt obligation market, which generated more demand for securitised loans and stretched quality guarantees even more thinly. Hedge funds joined the party, supported by leverage from banks that were exposing themselves to more and more risk – encouraged by analysts and regulators. Finally, generous compensation packages, initially from hedge funds and later from banks (who felt they had to compete for talent by matching these short-termist incentive structures) gave everyone a reason to perpetuate this upward spiral of make-believe.

In this new world of securitised and structured finance, the risk was spread in ways that were hard to measure or even understand. Since nobody was charged with 'connecting the dots' of evolving industry architecture, nobody foresaw the crash.

Using this big-picture perspective can help us create new industry architectures while avoiding excessive blame – or misplaced forgiveness – for the current downturn. It is important that policymakers take such a systemic view into account as they restructure this critical sector. As they do, they may want to reframe the pointless debate about 'too much' or 'too little' intervention of the state. States can institutionalise the rules of architectures; and markets are integral, but engineered, parts of architectures, shaping individual and collective behaviour. What financial services need now is a robust architecture, not one where the state simply pours in resources or micro-manages everything. To get it right, we must ensure both that the parts of the system make sense, and that the way to put them together is sustainable.

Changing industry architecture

Many sectors have changed dramatically during the past few years, reducing leaders to laggards and turning newcomers into giants. Consider the early days of computing, where the industry unbundled, vertically dis-integrating, changing the competitive dynamics and even the identity of the sector. IBM outsourced too much during the 1980s giving up critical business functions. Meanwhile, the Apple of the late 1980s was too integrated and closed, losing the battle for personal computing and allowing previously unknown companies to capture the key parts of its value proposition. Both organisations came close to failure.

Microsoft, by contrast, used shrewd agreements to maintain its position as a 'bottleneck', retaining the key parts of the computing value-added process and guaranteeing a foothold in the critical area of graphical user interface, operating system and pre-installed software. Companies such as Microsoft do not just work *in* a sector – they work *on* it, shaping the sector and ensuring that the future of the industry will fit their capabilities.

IBM and Apple's more recent history suggests that they, too, managed to overcome their previous failures by becoming more savvy managers of their sector's architecture. IBM's rebirth in the 1990s was based on an open, flexible model that focused on keeping the critical parts of customer handling and higher value-added sectors, while exiting the commoditised parts of the business.

Apple's return to dominance through the iPod was the result of a cleverly designed ecosystem: by controlling iTunes, design, the brand and pricing, Apple ensured it ruled the environment without needing to integrate most parts of the value chain. In other words, it turned itself into a bottleneck. Because its supplier relationships are so well designed, Apple does not need to manufacture any of the components of an iPod. It also fosters competition between the different 'complementors' – makers of speakers and iPod accessories, who agree to play by Apple's rules and create an installed base of compatible products. So, the company's success stems, in large part, from its ability to build a new industry architecture.

Even when no single company dominates a sector, profits migrate as industry architectures change. Consider the increasingly untenable position of large telecommunications operators, which have been challenged by new ways of making money and having to reposition themselves constantly vis-à-vis content providers, handset manufacturers and service providers. Or consider healthcare, where traditional pharmaceutical companies are having to change their value-adding activities as demands for personalised medicine and more advanced care change the landscape. The new winners will be the companies that manage to adapt, changing the way they make money. In every industry, success flows from the ability to adapt to (or reshape) industry architecture and your role within it.

Rethink your role, reshape the architecture – especially in a downturn

As downturn becomes recession and credit evaporates, other industry architectures are up for grabs. Recessions cause transformations in the way we do business. The 1970s downturn gave European and US manufacturers the chance to change their practices and reorganise their supply chains. The early 1990s recession helped spur the growth of outsourcing, and the IT slump at the start of this decade ushered in a new type of networked organisation and flexible workers.

When sectors are growing, everyone is busy making money. They carry on doing what they have always done, even if it is inefficient, and nobody wants to voice any doubts or change the sector. But when the going gets tough, companies are willing to consider entirely new ways of doing business, and established leaders may be unable to prevent changes in the structure of their sector.

Consider the UK construction sector, which was stable for decades and inefficient for a very long time. New ideas such as 'design for buildability' and 'design for cost minimisation' only took hold when the 1990s recession forced existing players to change their structures and span more parts of the value chain in order to survive.

Crisis means new industry architectures. That means new opportunities for those who can adapt and challenges for those who think that a downturn can only mean lower output, lay-offs and retrenchment. Customer needs are different in a downturn: consumption shifts from an aspirational, image-driven model to an emphasis on thrift and value, as we can see from the spike in sales of low-price retail chains such as Aldi, Lidl or Wal-Mart over the Christmas period in Europe and the US.

Business-to-business relationships are being redrawn, shifting the focus from growth to preserving cash. Capital markets are preoccupied with risk. And regulators are aiming for corporate survival at all costs, where once they sought competition. This is why downturns are associated with rapid changes in a sector's pecking order – a threat for those at the top and an opportunity for those hungry for success. So what should companies do?

Writing your rags-to-riches story

Adapting to a new reality, changing the way you do business or reshaping your industry's architecture is no mean feat. First, you need to work out how you can add value in the new environment. This requires realigning what the company does to match emerging needs. It means reconsidering how the organisation is structured, and how its financial and capital structure translates success into results.

To do this, you must clearly express why and how a company can add value, and explain how it can continue doing so as the downturn deepens and conditions change. You have to decide how to reposition the company in the sector, distinguishing between temporary lulls and profound cyclical changes, and consider what could be tenable in the future. You need to plan for the worst while plotting your course to emerge stronger from this difficult period.

You must also leverage the needs of other companies to gain a strategic and architectural advantage for tomorrow. As economic conditions change, companies that you deal with will develop new priorities; they will be less concerned about structuring their long-term plans or positions than preserving cash or addressing immediate needs. So, in exchange for accommodating their short-term requirements, you could build a relationship to enhance your long-term prospects. And consider how you can capitalise on cheap resources available today: most of the technology-based companies that were hiring in the wake of the 2001 stock market crash reaped handsome returns from the exceptional talent they could afford to lock in. Strategic recruiting of bright graduates now could lead, a few years down the road, to a formidable strength.

> " A downturn could be just the challenge you need to energise your business and restructure your sector "

You might also have the opportunity to occupy the niches that other companies are being forced to leave (especially in emerging markets). This is one of the reasons why some companies can grow in leaps and bounds during downturns and why established leaders are particularly vulnerable, even if they appear less prone to going under.

It is like judo as opposed to boxing: using rivals' weight to your advantage. Most of today's giants initially positioned themselves as allies of existing players, carving new business models, reshaping industry architectures and gradually improving their positions. They shaped their own long-term future by understanding and meeting the short-term needs of the companies around them.

Consider a company such as Velti, an upstart in the interface between mobile communications and advertising. It re-shapes the nature of the sector around it by updating its business model as the sector evolves, and shifting its compensation model to a results-driven structure, to preserve cash for its clients and reduce their perception of risk in a technology venture. Or consider more established players that capitalise on growth opportunities caused by the downturn, such as the hedge funds and private equity groups with plenty of cash that are starting to replace functions traditionally performed by investment banks. It is essential to redefine yourself as needs change.

But many companies do find themselves in crisis management mode. In order to move forward, they need to address the causes of diminished performance, not the symptoms. This, alas, does not come easy. In a crisis, organisations often resort to fire-fighting or papering over the cracks. They try to cut costs to deal with declining revenues, often spreading the pain equally across lines of business or functional divisions. Worse still, they might eliminate the areas that appear 'easy to cut' in the short-term, cashing in every investment regardless of its medium-term prospects. This risks throwing the baby out with the bathwater.

Instead, companies and their leaders need to recognise that changes in customers and markets require a wholesale rethink of their value proposition, business model or financial structure. Focusing on the basic questions of how value is added can help companies save themselves from a spiral of cost-cutting and lay-offs that ends in administration regardless.

Thinking about industry architectures can also help to dispel the doomy introspection that accompanies downturns. In tough times, everyone looks inwards, obsessing over redundancies, politics and re-organisation – losing touch with customers and the market just when they can least afford to. Finding a way to refocus on value, on what lies behind the financial results, could help to combat this dangerous tendency. It could be just the challenge you need to energise and awaken the talent in your business and restructure your company and your sector.

Companies that have the courage to do so, do much more than manage their operations and costs to return to profitability. They identify which parts of their business are viable and which are not, taking the crisis as an opportunity to take a strategic look at their future and that of their sector.

We know that companies do not change unless they are forced to, and that managers have used 'burning platforms' as an opportunity to reorganise from time immemorial. The good news is that no one needs convincing that the platform is burning. The flames are around our ears. What is important now is not to let a good crisis go to waste.

23

Why sustainability is still going strong

While philanthropic giving will suffer during the downturn, companies will find that sustainability remains a key component of long-term strategy. By **Daniel Vermeer** and **Robert Clemen**

I n the wake of the deepening economic crisis, many commentators are warning of the demise of corporate sustainability, the practice of balancing profit with the social and environmental impact of doing business. Companies obsessed with their own short-term survival, they suggest, cannot possibly support long-term, 'feel-good' initiatives to protect the environment or invest in community development.

We see things differently. The downturn will produce more integrated, strategic and value-creating sustainability efforts in many companies. While traditional corporate responsibility and philanthropic initiatives may suffer, core elements of the sustainability agenda will survive or even thrive in a re-ordered economy.

One aspect of sustainability that is alive and kicking, perhaps more so because of the economic crisis, is concern with corporate governance. Public perception and trust of large corporations have been seriously damaged. The downturn will keep pressure on companies and executives to rebuild that trust and they must show a renewed commitment to do business in ways that go far beyond adherence to legal requirements, incorporating decision making and reporting procedures that respect all stakeholders. Companies that fail to show such commitment will find themselves at risk when the economic conditions improve.

Concern with corporate governance is a fairly recent addition to a broader array of sustainability issues. Companies have been balancing economic, social and environmental objectives for much longer. In the 1970s, the earliest corporate sustainability efforts were developed to respond to new regulations in the US and Europe, and focused primarily on regulatory compliance and risk management. Environmental and social departments were designed as buffers, managing legal and regulatory obligations so the rest of the organisation could focus on making a profit. Many of the more successful companies have developed philanthropic programmes that direct a portion of corporate profits towards worthy causes, often through a corporate foundation created to support projects in communities where the company operates.

> **ff Coca-Cola's approach is not philanthropic, but is based on a realistic assessment of what is required to continue to operate 55**

But this philanthropic approach is bound to suffer in the current downturn. For example, the three big US automakers have historically subsidised a broad array of social and economic initiatives, especially in the Detroit area. However, in the light of the automakers' dismal economic prospects, local charities and non-profits expect corporate contributions to drop as much as 30 per cent in 2009.

Eco-efficiency

As companies have built sustainability capabilities and systems, generally under the broad title of 'eco-efficiency', it has become clear that sustainability management can contribute substantially to the bottom line by driving more efficient use of resources and reducing waste. For example, 3M's '3P' programme, which started in 1975 to identify specific efficiency projects, has led to about $1bn in cumulative savings.

In the current business environment, however, there are obvious reasons why companies might want to reduce their levels of investment in eco-efficiency. First, the economic crisis has dampened demand for many resources and, thus, reduced the costs of energy, raw materials and other natural resources. This has made the business case for investing in energy efficiency more difficult to make. Second, eco-efficiency efforts vary widely in the amount of upfront capital required. While most companies have significant opportunities to reduce resource use through better operational practices, opportunities that are more significant typically require greater investment. For cash-strapped companies, it may become difficult to justify immediate outlays in anticipation of savings in the long term.

So, the outlook for eco-efficiency is decidedly mixed, continuing in most companies, but focusing on lower-key and lower-cost measures.

Consumers, retailers and supply chains

Consumers continue to demand green products, and in some cases demand is growing. According to a study by the Fresh Ideas Group, a public relations firm, consumers in 2009 will be more conscious of product impacts but also more value-conscious. The best positioned products will produce immediate savings, such as efficient lighting, or yield multiple benefits, such as local food that is perceived to be both greener and healthier. Big-ticket items, such as hybrid cars, or products with hefty premiums for an environmental benefit, such as organic bedsheets, may be more difficult to shift off shelves.

Retailers with strong and growing sustainability ambitions should flourish. Perhaps the most visible example is Wal-Mart, the world's biggest retailer, which has announced several goals in the past few years, including zero waste, 100 per cent renewable energy use, 'sustainable products' and, most recently, new standards for the environmental and social performance of its suppliers. For the supplier, this could be a burden but it could also be seen as an opportunity.

Tesco, the UK retailer, has also raised the bar for its suppliers, most notably requiring certain products to provide labelling information about the product's carbon footprint.

Big retailers such as Wal-Mart and Tesco play important roles in educating consumers about the importance of sustainability and providing more affordable options in the marketplace. While we are still early in this process, there are encouraging signs that the retailer sustainability effect is real and is here to stay.

Sustainability as strategy

Changing economic and regulatory environments will lead more companies to adopt corporate strategies that include sustainability as a core issue. In their simplest form, such strategies will focus on helping a company's customers to cope with their own sustainability issues.

General Electric's Ecomagination programme is a good example. By developing and marketing products ranging from compact fluorescent light bulbs for homeowners to more efficient gas turbines for power-generating utilities, GE profits by providing ways for its customers to reduce their own operational costs.

The current economic crisis adds tension – customers with less cash to spend may reduce demand for such products. However, this appears to be primarily a financing issue. The companies that succeed may well be those that can help their customers finance purchases so the timing of cash outlays and operational savings are brought closer together.

Establishing sustainability as a core element of strategy is a much deeper problem. Companies will have to broaden their understanding of the system within which they operate, which includes a broad range of impinging factors, trends, forces and interactions. Developing this understanding will involve more than a conventional economic analysis.

In *The Necessary Revolution: How Individuals and Organisations Are Working Together to Create a Sustainable World*, Peter Senge of the Sloan School of Management, MIT reveals that companies will need a deep systems-based understanding of how the global economy, environment, society and geopolitics interact and affect the organisation. His work predates the current economic crisis, but it only strengthens his argument. Retailers and manufacturers must consider the possibility of severe upstream disruptions in supply and distributions chains, and at the same time grasp how economic and political conditions across the world will affect them. Add in volatility in energy and natural resources markets and potential disruptions in resource supply, and the importance of large-scale system-based comprehension becomes crucial for companies to succeed or, in some cases, simply survive.

Companies that are able to adapt will see that problems previously considered to be outside their sphere of influence actually fall within their purview. A good example is how Coca-Cola has dealt with water sustainability challenges. As water resources have become increasingly stressed and scarce in many parts of the world, Coca-Cola has begun to experience more conflicts with communities and other water users, most notably in India. Beginning in 2002, the company launched a thorough evaluation of its water use and associated risks, and developed a water sustainability programme that goes well beyond the traditional narrow focus on legal compliance and efficiency alone. As this work has evolved, Coca-Cola has increased its involvement in community efforts to ensure access to clean drinking water, watershed protection projects, especially in water-stressed regions, and efforts to mobilise the international community to anticipate and deal with ever more severe water crises worldwide. Coca-Cola's approach is not philanthropic, but rather based on a realistic assessment of what is required to continue to operate a beverage company in an increasingly water-stressed world.

Conclusion

Ultimately, sustainability in the 21st century will require companies to 'go deep, go wide, go local'.

'Going deep' means institutionalising sustainability into the company's DNA to the extent that it becomes part and parcel of strategy. 'Going wide' implies a full understanding of how sustainability impinges on every aspect of the organisation's value chain. Finally, 'going local' paradoxically goes hand-in-hand with globalisation, forcing companies to examine their global operations in order to identify and ameliorate specific local issues that affect the company's operations, customers, competitive position, brand image, political standing or any aspect of its ability to do business.

Adopting a phrase from John Ehrenfeld's *Sustainability by Design*, we see sustainability as flourishing within limits. Companies that are able to grasp the system within which they operate and the limits and requirements the system imposes will be the ones to flourish in the future business environment.

Time to bring real shareholders back on board

Failures at big financial institutions underline the need for strong corporate boards with industry expertise that challenge a company's top executives. By **Paul Strebel**

I n the scramble to design a new regulatory architecture, more should be said about reforming the requirements for corporate boards. No matter how sophisticated the new regulatory regime is, creative minds and egos will find ways round it. Boards with teeth are the final rampart against managerial folly and egos that run amok.

Looking at what has happened to the world's largest financial institutions, two differences distinguish the boards of the better performers: a significant number of board members with industry expertise, or a governance structure, that prevented the emergence of an entrenched, dominant CEO or chairperson.

Citigroup, Merrill Lynch, UBS, Washington Mutual, Fannie Mae, Freddie Mac, AIG, Lehman Brothers, Bear Stearns, ABN Amro, Fortis, RBS and HBOS all had boards with very little, if any, financial markets expertise. Though their board members were eminent in their particular fields, without industry expertise they could not see through the triple A-rated collateralised debt obligations, identify the build-up of risk and act as powerful sparring partners to the CEO and top executives. By contrast, companies including Deutsche Bank, Allianz, Credit Suisse, BNP Paribas, Unicredit and Goldman Sachs had financial markets expertise on their boards and had writedowns and balance sheet problems that were much less severe than the banks mentioned above.

The data from the current crisis strongly suggest that, at board level, especially in an industry with complex derivative and structured products, expertise weighs more than diversity. In remarks to the Swiss Federal Banking Commission on the breakdown in its risk management, Marcel Rohner, who was appointed CEO of UBS in August, said the bank had missed the bigger picture, by relying too much on its risk management process: 'The problem was not a failure to appreciate complexity, but rather the opposite. It was a lack of simplicity and critical perspective, which prevented the right questions from being asked while there was still time.'

❝❝ Boards dominated by professional board members, CEOs and former CEOs of other groups have failed dismally ❞❞

Boards dominated by professional board members, CEOs and former CEOs of other companies have failed dismally. They bring no industry expertise to the table, have little of their own wealth at stake, too easily identify with the CEO/chairperson and go along with an increasing concentration of power at the top. At the financial institutions with the biggest losses, the lack of industry expertise on the board was almost always associated with a dominant CEO and/or chairperson.

Avoiding this concentration of power and getting the board to align top management with shareholders' interests requires board members who are the true representatives of the shareholders. Nobody with meaningful money on the table is inclined to let others play recklessly with their equity. The best examples of good governance are on boards with partners or shareholders who have a big percentage of their wealth at stake.

On a widely held, truly representative shareholder board, the majority of seats would be reserved for the largest shareholders and elected representatives of the minority shareholders. The role of the nominating committee would be to apportion the seats, call for and make the nominations with a preference for industry expertise and run the voting procedure where necessary. This is similar to the role played by the nominating committee in Sweden, typically made up of large investors. A minority of seats would be reserved to bring in other critical stakeholders or mandated expertise to the table where needed.

A truly representative shareholder board would be fractious and unstable at times, when shareholder blocks have divergent interests. However, this would be much healthier than artificial harmony among non-representative board members, or the boardroom dramas that occur when unrepresented large shareholders try to force their way on to the board. A truly representative board would quickly see where those with the ownership majority want to take the company. Minority shareholders would have representatives to raise the red flag, or turn to regulators, if their interests are abused.

Diverse boards of notables cannot represent the owners adequately. It is time to put real shareholders back on the board

New models for the future

Social entrepreneurs show how companies can turn profits while improving conditions in poor countries. By **Christian Seelos**

B oom times provide companies with abundant short-term opportunities. During downturns, however, opportunities seemingly 'dry up' and managers need to explore new strategies to enact future business success.

Unfortunately, we do not have good recipes for building the right organisational competencies that fit and support strategic positions in tomorrow's markets. An alternative approach is to replicate and rejuvenate existing competencies in emerging economies using 'symbiotic business models' and thereby create new markets. This article provides some practical strategic pointers on how this can be done.

In some countries, particularly those with large-scale poverty, there may be no existing market to enter. Thus, a decision might hinge more on how to build markets and the necessary institutional structures.

In these circumstances, institutions supporting market exchange, such as property rights or specialist intermediaries, are often weak or absent. As a result, the conventional sectors in which entrepreneurs and companies compete are either poorly developed or lacking. As economist Douglass North has pointed out: 'Third world countries are poor because the institutional constraints define a set of pay-offs to political/economic activity that do not encourage productive activity.'

But recent research by myself and Johanna Mair has revealed the important role of 'social entrepreneurs'. These are individuals who help build institutions and innovative business models in emerging economies – the basis for competitive and productive markets and sustainable development. Social entrepreneurs have often worked for decades to build the resources and competencies needed to overcome the obstacles associated with serving the poor efficiently. But because these leaders focus primarily on social objectives, their resources and competencies are often under valued from an economic or business perspective.

In contrast to the traditional 'bottom of the pyramid' (BoP) perspective, we propose that companies are better off partnering with social entrepreneurs and providing scale to the business models already being used by them. This approach allows companies to access valuable local resources, leading to profitable market positions and encouraging long-term development. This model creates profits that are generated by combining local resources with existing corporate competencies to serve the growing middle-class or other higher-income customers locally and internationally.

The banking industry believed it was impossible to make money through the provision of micro-loans to the poor, but the Grameen Bank, founded in Bangladesh by Muhammad Yunus in 1976, proved the industry wrong. For 2006, the year Mr Yunus received the Nobel Peace Prize, Grameen reported $725m in disbursed loans and $20m profits. Microfinance institutions such as Compartamos Banco in Mexico have reported returns on equity of as high as 40 per cent, sparking debate over the legitimacy of such profit levels from serving the poor.

In the 1990s, when the telecommunications industry believed it was impossible to make money serving poor customers in Bangladesh, the Norwegian telecoms business Telenor banded together with Mr Yunus to prove the industry wrong again.

GrameenPhone, a commercial company, was operated by experienced Telenor managers with the aim of maximising financial returns by exploiting their competencies of building mobile telephony infrastructure and marketing to middle- and higher-income customers in urban centres.

GrameenTelecom was set up to manage the interface between Telenor and Grameen's microfinance business model to scale up Grameen's capacity to create jobs for the rural poor. This was necessary because the real bottleneck to scale for Grameen was not the capacity to provide finance, but to create opportunities for productive jobs to enable the poor to make good use of the loans.

A guide to building symbiotic models

Activities	Rationale	Remark
Scan prospective countries or regions for companies with business models able to serve the poor, particularly if the product or service can be linked to achieving the United Nations Millennium Development Goals (MDGs), which aim to improve social and economic conditions in the world's poorest countries.	The number and types of organisations may indicate crucial institutional and structural aspects of the environment. Links to MDGs may indicate opportunities for accessing development resources and funds.	Organisations such as Ashoka or the Schwab Foundation which promote social entrepreneurship provide useful information. Poverty reduction strategy papers may also help to understand country development and funding priorities.
Understand the strategic objectives, culture and structures of these organisations.	Identify potential partners through attributes such as size, scope or longevity. Learn to speak their language and respect their identity to overcome their potential lack of trust.	Social entrepreneurship is now taught in many business schools. Case studies (available at www.caseplace.org) are helpful as are meetings such as the World Economic Forum in Davos.
Build relationships with a number of organisations as early as possible.	Pre-empt access to their resources. Help to build up scale and scope. Build mutual trust.	These organisations provide opportunities for hands-on training and employee-development schemes. They could constitute a portfolio of small investments as options for building new markets.
Identify an important bottleneck in the partner organisation's business model that limits its ability to achieve strategic goals. Build your for-profit business model around providing the constraining element.	Provide capacity to an existing model that will enable an easy interface between partners. The bottleneck element to the business models of both partners aligns intentions and enables easy performance measures.	Business modelling helps to identify bottlenecks and design the overall model across partner organisations.
Start your business model design process by thinking about replicating your existing competencies for foreign markets or to build new product markets.	Existing capabilities allow products to be brought to market more quickly and eliminate complexity and uncertainty.	Corporations create real benefits from their unique resources and capabilities. Being clear on which competencies allow you to act at the bottom of BoP is a healthy reality check and may avoid experiments that have limited chances for success.
Ensure that the business model supports an increase in the real income of people.	Increase in real income will improve the ability of poor people to make consumption choices and expand the customer base for companies.	Include job creation as an element and development driver in your business model. Work with organisations whose core strategic objective is job creation.

Activities	Rationale	Remark
Monitor the dynamics of the environment and/or the development of the partner company's overall model and strategic objectives.	Quickly address emerging threats to the sustainability of the alliance. Evaluate the possibility of building relationship-specific assets or asset configurations. Do not become a bottleneck to your partner's future development.	Corporate intelligence and communication from diverse stakeholders may help monitor relevant developments in the political, social, technical and environmental arena. Share insights with your partners in joint strategy sessions.

GrameenPhone began operating in 1997, was profitable by 2000 and had passed 6m subscribers and held 60 per cent of market share by 2006. It is now one of Bangladesh's biggest private companies and creates significant profits for Telenor.

Meanwhile, by 2006, GrameenTelecom had created more than 250,000 jobs for micro entrepreneurs whom it calls 'Village Phone Ladies', poor rural women who generate income by providing a village phone service.

The joint venture with Grameen was critical for Telenor for a number of reasons: it safeguarded the company's reputation against the widespread corruption in Bangladesh; it provided Telenor with the trusted and widely known Grameen brand, facilitating marketing efforts and establishing local legitimacy in a short time and at very low cost; and the decision to provide scale to Grameen's model of job creation for the poor, instead of just serving urban middle class customers, allowed Telenor to access development funds that absorbed much of the financial risk and enabled fast country-wide proprietary infrastructure development at a low cost – a strong basis for sustained competitive advantage.

Of course, economic success depends on the ability of managers to integrate resources into a business model that creates greater value than the cost of the resources. Organisations with primarily social objectives, such as those led by social entrepreneurs, can be a source of economically undervalued resources and capabilities.

The case of Telenor demonstrates how a company can provide scale to these organisations, generating greater social value from established business models that work in a local context. In return, social entrepreneurs can provide companies with valuable resources to build the for-profit side and achieve the corporate partner's financial strategic objectives.

Symbiotic business models

Managing the social and for-profit elements in separate organisations eliminates confusion over non-aligned strategic objectives and the potential mismatch of competencies and organisational cultures.

Every partner in this model is better off if the other partner maximises their private benefit. Thus, Telenor gains revenues and potential consumers from the efforts of Grameen to build jobs, which helps Telenor to maximise its financial returns. Similarly, Grameen can create more jobs when Telenor builds up its business model quickly and is able to sustain provision of discounted connectivity to Grameen. Hence, 'symbiotic business models': the joint value created is far greater than the sum of the two organisations operating in isolation.

The Telenor/Grameen case also demonstrates how several of the strategic challenges of traditional BoP recommendations can be overcome. The inherent complexity for large companies of having to create multiple strategies for different income levels is avoided by having two separate organisations utilising different business models. The for-profit model is largely based on replicating or redeploying existing corporate capabilities rather than building new ones.

The table on the left summarises some practical and conceptual pointers for developing business models that satisfy corporate needs for growth and returns as well as the needs of the poor.

Inspired corporate strategy means 'shaping a desired future' not just reacting to short-term changes. Market positions that explicitly target the challenges of sustainable development can thereby become an essential part of corporate strategies.

chapter

26

Sovereign wealth revalued

Despite claims that they pursue political agendas, sovereign wealth
funds usually add long-term value. By **Nuno Fernandes** and **Arturo Bris**

L ack of confidence in financial markets has driven investors and
funds away from corporations. As balance sheets deteriorate, companies are in need of more and more capital, which investors are
not willing to provide. In this setting, sovereign wealth funds (SWFs)
have emerged as the funding source of the next few years. According to
the Sovereign Wealth Fund Institute, SWFs manage $3,000bn. To put this
figure into perspective, the hedge fund and private equity markets combined account for less than $2,000bn. Some estimates suggest that SWFs
will manage more than $10,000bn by 2015.

However, SWFs' investment strategies and potential political agendas
remain controversial. In this article, we move beyond the strategic discussion and provide evidence on the impact of SWFs on company valuation,
based on research done at IMD that covers more than 20,000 SWF holdings across 7,000 companies and covers funds' stock holding in 58
countries' stock markets.

How do SWFs operate?

In principle, SWFs invest in equities with the purpose of maximising the
return on a country's reserves. By taking sizeable stakes in corporations,
they perform a desirable corporate governance role that should be welcomed by other shareholders. Unlike other controlling shareholders,

SWFs pursue nothing but share return maximisation. Plus, they are usually long-term and well-governed investors, so managers should feel the pressure to perform, even if SWFs have – until recently – been reluctant to sit on boards of directors.

On the other hand, being powerful investors, there is no reason why we should not expect SWFs to expropriate minority shareholders. Concentrated ownership may be associated with the extraction of private benefits of control and, therefore, should be value decreasing.

With noteworthy exceptions (for example, the Norway Government Pension Fund) SWFs are opaque in their objectives and strategies. It has been argued that they hinder competition because the industries in which they invest are not open to foreign investment in their own countries. Politicians' response in general suggests a fear of hidden political agendas. For example, Nicolas Sarkozy, French president, said in early 2008: 'I believe... in globalisation but I don't accept that certain sovereign wealth funds can buy anything here and our own capitalists can't buy anything in their countries. I demand reciprocity before we open Europe's barriers.'

Where do SWFs invest?

SWFs invest in virtually all countries in the developed world, and a few emerging market economies. As market players, they are certainly a driving force, holding positions in almost one-fifth of companies worldwide. The typical position taken by an SWF is not a controlling stake. On average, an SWF takes 0.74 per cent of the shares outstanding in a company. In dollar terms, the average position is $46.3m. Indeed, their level of control only reaches 50 per cent in less than 1 per cent of their investments.

The average company held by an SWF has total assets of $229m, annual sales growth of 15 per cent, and a leverage ratio of 24 per cent. In terms of visibility indicators, the average company is tracked by 13 analysts and 32 per cent of its sales are international. Compared with typical companies in the global market, companies held by SWFs are significantly larger, more liquid and have proven records of profitable growth. Companies held by SWFs also tend to have significantly higher institutional ownership and analyst coverage than the rest.

SWFs are often opportunistic. They step into companies when their stock prices fall. They are also more inclined to invest in countries where legal protection of investors is stronger. In other words, they may bring in good governance, but only to the extent that the legal regime guarantees a minimum protection to their investment. As with other non-sovereign investment vehicles (Calpers, the California state pension fund, for example), corporate governance considerations are, therefore, important determinants of SWFs investment strategies.

Despite their preference for visible companies and demand for shares with high analyst coverage, SWFs do not reveal any strong demand for companies that belong to the major share indices such as the Morgan Stanley Composite Index. Unlike regular mutual funds, SWFs have no business concerns in terms of performance and flows. The money that flows into the fund is independent of its performance (or any bench-marking), and relies heavily on the health of the domestic economies of each of their countries. It is often argued that SWFs invest in western companies as a means of gaining corporate intelligence, but SWFs do not display any preference for high-tech or research and development-intensive companies.

Impact on company value

Academic research has shown that the identity of a company's investors determines market valuations. If we agree that market valuations approximate accurately the fundamental values, this indicates that investors can affect company performance either by direct control or by conditioning the company's financial policies, and, ultimately, its operating strategy. Institutional ownership (particularly foreign) in general is associated with higher company valuations. SWFs are both large and foreign, so, in principle, they should encompass higher market valuations.

> **In the year when an SWF invests in a company, the ratio of the group's market value to its book value rises 15 per cent**

Indeed, the valuation impact of SWFs is sizeable. Our econometric analysis shows that in the year when an SWF invests in a company, the ratio of the market value of the company to its book value increases 15 per cent. Furthermore, the impact of SWFs goes beyond that of the typical institutional investor: the market pays, on average, a much higher premium for companies in which SWFs have a stake than companies owned by general institutional investors.

Benefits of SWF ownership

- SWFs can be more proactive in the takeover market and block value-reducing acquisitions by the companies they invest in. Because of their interest in share returns, SWFs avoid strategies that purely pursue value-destroying consolidation and scale.

- SWFs increase the takeover premiums in the companies in which they invest. In late 2008, Norway's Government Pension Fund opposed a bid by MidAmerican Energy Company (a unit of Warren Buffett's Berkshire Hathaway) for Constellation, in which the pension fund had a 4.8 per cent stake. MidAmerican's bid was backed by Constellation's management itself. However, Norway's SWF considered the price insufficient and has since brought MidAmerican to court. As this episode shows, powerful, non-controlling shareholders can exert external pressure.

- SWFs can act as efficient internal corporate governance mechanisms, bridging any gap between shareholders and the top executive. As a substitute for the legal system, one expects the value effect of SWFs to be larger when they invest in companies from countries with a weaker legal system. However, our analysis of the past five years shows that the SWF premium that we report above is the same regardless of the level of investor protection in the country of origin.

- Unlike other types of institutional investors, SWFs provide guaranteed capital in case of future funding needs and, therefore, reduce the uncertainty regarding the company's future financing ability. There are two characteristics of SWFs that make them more desirable than regular institutional investors: they are larger and they do not invest heavily in equities. As SWFs have access to massive funds, the market rewards the unlimited access to capital of the companies in which they invest. Current estimates suggest that SWFs are still significantly underexposed to equities, compared with regular pension funds or other institutional investors. The expectation is, therefore, that SWFs will gradually increase their exposure to equities in the coming years (to about 40 per cent).

- SWFs make companies more valuable because they reduce companies' cost of capital as a result of their commanding lower risk premiums. The opportunity cost of sovereign funds is to invest in risk-free instruments such as US bonds, as was their common practice in the 1980s. Furthermore, relative to their size, a single SWF stake represents a small percentage of their total assets anyway (the typical fund in the sample invests in more than 100 stocks), and the marginal investor of the companies in which they invest becomes a more global, international, less risk-averse investor.

- SWFs provide valuable political connections. Brazil has recently established its own SWF, with the stated objective of buffering the country from the global financial crisis and helping Brazilian companies to boost trade and expand overseas. It is likely that such international expansion is spurred by the Brazilian government's appeal with multinationals and other regulators.

The controversy surrounding SWFs is more political than financial. SWF ownership is usually positively valued by the market, with a premium amounting to about 15 per cent of company value. This suggests that, contrary to claims that SWFs expropriate investors and pursue political agendas, they, in fact, contribute to long-term shareholder value creation and bring about larger value increases than other institutional investors.

China and India take on the multinationals

Western multinationals have established themselves in both countries but could their dominance be under threat from ambitious home-grown challengers? By **Pankaj Ghemawat** and **Thomas M. Hout**

What will the ranks of the world's leading multinational corporations (MNCs) look like 25–50 years from now? And what will be the effect of the rebalancing of economic activity towards China and India, in particular, if they continue to grow rapidly and regain some of the share of gross domestic product that they ceded in the 19th and most of the 20th centuries?

At one extreme, one might imagine companies from these and other emerging markets crowding out ones from advanced economies: what has been dubbed the decline of the west and the rise of the rest. At the other, one could conceive of the companies from emerging markets continuing to be confined to marginal positions, with a few exceptions of the sort that we are already starting to see. Which of these extremes is likely to prove closer to the mark?

China and India present nearly ideal conditions for getting an early look at outcomes in the competition between developed economy MNCs and emerging market challengers. Both are large, inviting markets and have already produced serious competitors to older multinationals.

At the same time, India and especially China are now open to foreign competition in most key industries, making them highly attractive to MNCs, which appear increasingly aggressive and long-term in their investment time horizons in those markets. China and India account for more than two-thirds of all new research and development centres established by multinationals in recent years. Multinationals' total incoming capital investment into China and India combined dwarfs the amount flowing into other emerging economies.

Moreover, the markets and operating environments of China and India are radically different from multinationals' home markets, making possible a wide range of competitive encounters and outcomes. For example, both have several layers of product and customer segments that reward different approaches from competitors, making it possible for both local challengers and patient MNCs to find starting places and, over time, compete more directly as they migrate towards each other. Finally, outbound foreign direct investment by Chinese and Indian companies, while much discussed, is still very limited relative to both the size of the targeted foreign markets and domestic gross fixed capital formation, and is focused on a few sectors (particularly energy and metals). In addition, recent outflows spiked with the global credit bubble, and are likely to fall sharply in the medium term. It is in the domestic market that most challengers are going head to head with established MNCs.

Industry influences

There is plenty of admiring discussion of specific Indian and Chinese companies, with India's TCS, Infosys, and other software groups, and Haier, Pearl River Piano and Huawei from China cited repeatedly. But we want to go beyond this handful of examples to look more systematically at the unfolding competitive situation between MNCs and Indian and Chinese challengers.

We have the most detailed data on these questions for MNC-Chinese company competition in China, covering 33 modern industries. Chinese companies occupy the top two or three spots in 10 of these industries in China, multinationals in 10 and overseas Chinese in three. In the other 10, leadership depends on the segment, with Chinese typically leading lower performance, lower price point segments and MNCs leading in higher performance, higher price point ones.

The type of industry matters. MNCs tend to dominate industries in which R&D and advertising represent relatively high percentages of sales, and Chinese companies tend to dominate in industries where these measures are low. The first type tends to move at relatively high speed – fast rates of new product introduction, frequent technological advances, escalating customer demands, or frequent refreshing of the brand message. Examples of companies and industries of this type include Applied Materials and Tokyo Electron in semi-conductor-making equipment; Apple and Sony in advanced consumer electronics; Procter & Gamble and L'Oréal in personal care products; and Coca-Cola and Pepsi in beverages. Furthermore, MNCs are generally not losing these positions and, in some cases, are strengthening them.

> " Multinationals' global balance sheets, cash flows and share prices will hold up better than those of challengers "

In contrast, Chinese companies tend to lead in slower-moving businesses where product capability and design change less often, broad distribution is critical, customer needs change less frequently, production cost is a high percentage of price, or factory capital-intensity is high. Examples include Pearl River and Beijing Xinghai in pianos; Sichuan Changhong, Konka and TCL in tube-type television sets; Mengniu and Yili in dairy products; and Haier and Rongsheng Kelon in home appliances. These Chinese leaders are the survivors of fast-growth rivalries with other Chinese producers, where the basis of competition has been price, product reliability, production capacity growth and distribution.

Similar patterns show up in the 10 industries where leading depends on segment characteristics. Advanced product segments such as, for example, clean, high-performance diesel engines, the latest generation of telecom switches, leading-edge food packaging equipment, upscale autos and so on are led by MNCs, while less advanced, older versions of products are led by Chinese producers.

While India was relatively open during colonial times, independence in 1947 brought a shift to self-sufficiency and socialism. It was only in 1991 that it re-opened to foreign competition, and even then in many respects to a lesser extent than China. It is, therefore, less ideal for observing the competitive outcomes of MNCs versus challengers. Nevertheless, data on 79 manufacturing industries in India show that in the years after India started to open up in the early 1990s, MNCs, as in China, performed better in faster-moving businesses and worse in slower-moving or capital-intensive commodity businesses.

Three elements of strategy leverage

There are, of course, exceptions to these tendencies, and in an article published in Harvard Business Review last November, we focused on deviations from the patterns described above. The three kinds of methods MNCs and emerging challengers use to tilt outcomes in their favour are: by aggressively moving into new, fast-growing segments; better managing the convergence in costs across advanced and emerging markets; and reworking the value chain. However, here we want to focus on the patterns described above, not least because they also show up in other emerging markets. More generally, R&D- and advertising-intensity are the most robust markers, across country markets, of MNC presence.

Based on this pattern, which we have termed the AAA triangle, there seems to be a simple way of looking at the evolving rivalry between MNCs and their challengers. Each type of company has radically different strengths and weaknesses of position based on where they come from, how they are managed, and the specific capabilities and business positions they have built.

MNCs typically start with advantages in terms of marketing and technological know-how; and they can circulate this know-how globally and adapt it to local markets. More broadly, MNCs can be characterised as starting with an advantage in aggregating or achieving cross-border economies of scale and scope on the basis of their market positions and broad experience with products, processes, advanced technologies, customers, channels, supplier networks, partners, regulators and so on across the world, as well as the generally greater resources available to them.

Local challengers, in contrast, often base their cross-border strategies on leading positions in large home markets and operations well-adapted to the local context, for example Haier and Huawei in China and Bharat Forge and Ranbaxy in India. These companies prevail at home by adapting to what are often severe domestic operating conditions – a large population of rural poor, weak distribution, unreliable suppliers, uneven infrastructure and so on. Reflecting their less developed home markets, these challengers tend to have fewer, more standardised product and service offerings, in contrast to established MNCs' differing regional product lines and even brand positions.

The example of the Indian software companies, however, remind us that some challengers are born global rather than local; they start out by trying to project competitive advantages across borders, rather than domestically. The most likely source of cross-border advantage for any Chinese or Indian company at an early stage in its organisational development will be low costs at home, not just for workers, but for materials, construction and even spartan management practices – an arbitrage strategy.

These different starting positions translate into the three basic elements of strategy which we call the 'AAA triangle' for companies engaging internationally:

■ **Aggregation:** overcoming differences across markets to achieve cross-border economies of scale and scope;

■ **Adaptation:** adjusting to differences in conditions to achieve greater local responsiveness;

■ **Arbitrage:** exploiting differences (for example, cost or product standards) as a source of value creation.

This way of thinking about sources of advantage in cross-border competition suggests a way of visualising MNC and challenger interactions.

Figure 27.1 visualises a race towards the middle or beyond, even though neither side is likely to give up entirely on its initial types of advantage. In this race, effective MNCs operating in India or China adapt to these unique environments and work to neutralise any cost disadvantages against local competitors. This takes organisational patience, attitude changes and considerable investment in these local markets. For example, P&G in China and Unilever in India have localised their managements, broadened product lines to address needs and driven deep into rural markets by creating new distribution channels. Ogilvy & Mather, the advertising agency, has partnered with the Communist Youth League of China for market research. And on the supply side, LG in India and Nokia in China have both used huge production scale and sophistication to level the cost playing field against local producers.

But the MNC must maintain aggregation as its primary strength against emerging challengers, whose evolution they have considerable power to influence. This means taking new products, technology, customer knowledge, sales propositions, brand management, upgraded employee skills and so on from one market to another. Innovation by MNCs is a major reason why lower cost does not always prevail. Great multinationals do not give up on earning price premiums in emerging markets.

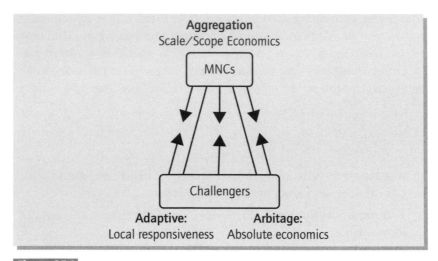

Aggregation
Scale/Scope Economics

MNCs

Challengers

Adaptive: **Arbitage:**
Local responsiveness Absolute economics

Figure 27.1

In contrast, the typical challenger seeking a presence in the MNC's home market or other markets where the MNC is present needs to build aggregation strength by developing deeper customer knowledge, local partnerships, global branding and so on. Another asset that has to be cultivated is corporate reputation, as illustrated by recent scandals ranging from Chinese dairy foods producer Sanlu's tainted milk powder to Satyam Computer Service's alleged $1bn fraud in India. Moreover, studies, such as the recent report by Transparency International, reveal that Chinese and Indian companies are perceived as most prone to pay bribes overseas. The scandals also highlight the need for professional management. Building up all these intangibles takes a great deal of time and money, and while acquisitions can help to substitute the latter for the former, the record to date illustrates that they also carry significant risks for novices.

Challengers must also move up the arbitrage ladder at home by upgrading its workers and value propositions, especially since the arbitrage opportunity at home is no longer reserved for domestic companies. Thus, in software services, western competitors such as IBM and Accenture have responded to the explosive profitability and growth of TCS, Infosys and other India-focused competitors by building up their own operations in India, lowering their costs as well as raising those of their competitors. TCS is responding effectively, increasing revenue per employee from less than $15,000 in 1990 to more than $50,000 today (and profit per employee from $2,000 to more than $10,000). This record reflects growing aggregation: emphasis on large projects, cross-selling 'solutions' and integrated delivery to one worldwide service standard from a global network of delivery centres.

Challengers need to be careful in going head-to-head with MNCs. Thus, Ranbaxy, formerly India's largest pharmaceutical company, got into trouble partly because its litigiousness cost it valuable collaborative opportunities with foreign pharma companies and, ironically, ultimately forced it into the arms of one of them. In other situations, the optimal response may not be to attack or to ally but to avoid established MNCs, at least in the short-to-medium run, by focusing on undeserved segments, such as Haier's focus on compact refrigerators; or focusing on newer ones, as Huawei has done in broadband telephony; or focusing on emergent segments or industries, as Suzlon of India is doing in wind energy (although it is currently hobbled by product problems).

Some challengers are not looking to internationalise or have an attribute that renders aggregation unnecessary. For example, home-grown websites Baidu and Taobao displaced early multinational leaders Google and Ebay in China by cleverly adapting to local customer needs but are not likely to challenge outside China. And Russian energy group Gazprom does not need to operate outside Russia to retain its advantage.

The past as a prelude to the future

It would be a mistake to interpret rapid growth in China and India as a guarantee that companies from those countries will emerge in large numbers as full-fledged MNCs. Adaptation may be a tall order for MNCs, but aggregation for challengers is equally or more difficult. And in technology- and advertising-intensive industries, few challengers will make it and most of those will grow to look much like today's multinationals.

There are two significant differences between today's competitive situation between established and aspiring multinationals and a generation ago, when Japanese companies caught many western MNCs by surprise. First, the Chinese and Indian economies are not only big and growing but essentially open, with some notable exceptions, to MNCs. Even Indian politics has shifted to favour at least partial modernisation.

The other difference is the readiness of MNCs. Twenty-five years ago, they had ageing product lines, no quality programmes, no sense of emerging markets' importance, and kept their rising management stars home. Today this has changed significantly, so that when Jeffrey Immelt, General Electric chief executive, said he was expecting 60 per cent of his revenue growth to come from emerging markets in the next 10 years, no one batted an eyelid.

Current recession and credit conditions do not change our findings. China and India will still grow while developed markets stand still or shrink, and emerging market currencies will most likely depreciate against developed market ones. But MNCs are now firmly embedded into China and India and enjoying these advantages. And their global balance sheets, cash flows and share prices will hold up better than those of challengers.

So we have our doubts about MNCs from emerging countries crowding out established ones. Instead, we see both types of companies as trying to move towards the centre of the AAA Triangle. We know the multinationals' game plan. It has unquestionably sharpened and evolved over the years to take account of new markets, offshoring, partnering, 24/7 communications and so on, but it has not invented fundamentally new ways of being a multinational. Emerging market challengers do not appear to have found fundamentally new paths to becoming multinationals.

Cross-border advantage will continue to come in the three forms we have described, and the job of management will continue to be to emphasise a subset of them while doing an adequate job on the remainder through appropriate management of tensions and trade-offs. And while many challengers will not succeed (or will be bought out), the interplay between them and established MNCs is bound to be one of the more interesting competitive stories to unfold over the next few decades.

Box A

Current business models of multinationals in China

Global brand leaders (e.g. Procter & Gamble, Kodak) Come in on the strength of premium brands, then extend to lower price points and second- and third-tier cities. Build full organisations in China as brand businesses require the biggest presence.

Global networkers (e.g. Cummins, LG) Establish China position in a high-performance part of the market. Source globally from a broad design and production network. China is not the only good place to produce standard products at low cost.

Hybrids (e.g. Li&Fung, Hon Hai) Use China as production base, mainly keeping higher-value design and marketing at home while transferring the simpler of these tasks gradually to China.

Pure technology leaders (e.g. Tokyo Electron, Intel) Leading position in China driven by unique technology. Very limited value added in China.

Service network builders (e.g. Otis Elevator, FedEx) Global leaders establishing a China-wide service network that draws on global expertise and links. Capitalise on Chinese competitors' inexperience in modern service mentality.

Personalising risk management

Why is it that very smart executives can sometimes make extraordinarily poor risk decisions? By **Julian Birkinshaw** and **Huw Jenkins**

This question has bothered observers of the business world for generations, but in the past 18 months it has gained extra importance as we try to make sense of the implosion of the financial services industry.

Of course, the problem of poor risk management is not confined to banking: sectors as different as oil and gas, pharmaceuticals and telecommunications have all experienced their share of poorly judged risks. But the banking industry, and the credit crisis in particular, provides a rich context for understanding where risk management goes wrong and how it can be improved.

In the years leading up to the credit crisis, most financial services companies focused on the formalisation of risk management, by developing multi-stage procedures with many signatories to evaluate and adjudicate on what risks were worth taking. They also relied on externalisation of risk management to a large degree – the use of expertise and approval from outside parties such as auditors, regulators and credit ratings agencies. We suggest that in future they need to give more attention to the personalisation of risk management. This requires greater quality of insight, greater personal accountability and a stronger support culture for risk management.

Personalisation of risk management does not mean throwing out the traditional systems and support structures. Rather, it means a subtle shift in emphasis from the management of a portfolio of risks to the underwriting of individual risk decisions. This approach is relevant across all sectors of the economy, not just to the world of financial services companies.

How do companies manage risk

Risk management requires companies to balance two distinct types of risks: the 'false positive' risk associated with investing in a potential opportunity that does not transpire; and the 'false negative' risk associated with failing to act on an opportunity that did transpire.

The consequences of false positive and false negative errors are very different. For example, if an oil and gas company is extremely cautious about investing in new oilfields, it can generally avoid costly false-positive mistakes in the form of dry wells, but it risks leaving money on the table that other competitors can pick up.

So how do companies manage risk? How do they bring to bear the necessary level of knowledge and expertise on difficult decisions? And how do they ensure that individuals act in the best interests of the company, rather than themselves? Historically, the answer to these questions was bureaucracy. While the term is often used in a pejorative sense, bureaucracy has benefits: namely, it encourages the development of formal rules and procedures that transcend individual idiosyncracies and historical orthodoxies. However, it also has many unwanted side effects: it can become overly rigid and specialised, it discourages individual thought, and it can lead to depersonalisation and a lack of ownership on the part of employees.

It is this last effect that is most salient here. As companies grow, they need to build formal systems to generate economies of scale and scope, but they need to balance that with the agility, personal accountability and freedom of expression that comes from a small, more entrepreneurial environment. While this point is often made in the context of innovation and creativity, it is just as valid in the management of risk.

Consider, for example, the winners and losers in the credit crisis. While there were certainly some notable failures among small players such as hedge funds, the big losses were borne disproportionately by the very large banks. This was partly because small financial services companies did not have the credit ratings or balance sheets to carry the so-called 'super senior' tranches of the collateralised debt obligations that ultimately got the big investment banks into trouble. But it was also partly because the decision makers were close to the action, highly knowledgeable and personally accountable for the outcomes of their decisions. As one leading hedge fund executive commented: 'We have robust informal systems, we communicate naturally, and we develop our own views on what risks to take. We get a return on our judgment.' This is the exact opposite of a bureaucratic system, and a world away from the thousand-person strong risk functions that some of the large investment banks had built up during the boom years.

> ❝ In the credit crunch, the largest banks lost out disproportionately compared with smaller players ❞

To put it another way, there are three complementary approaches to managing risk in large companies.

- Formalisation involves using formal procedures and rules to evaluate and adjudicate on what risks are worth taking.

- Externalisation involves making use of the expertise and seal of approval provided by third parties – some required by law (auditors and regulators), others optional but widely used (credit ratings agencies). Both of these approaches are manifestations of bureaucracy – the former controlled by the company's management, the latter controlled by third parties.

- Personalisation involves pushing the responsibility for evaluating and making a judgment on risk to those individuals who are making decisions.

While all three are necessary and used to varying degrees all the time, the recent evidence in banking and elsewhere suggests that we need to redress the balance back towards personalisation, especially in large companies.

Goldman Sachs, one of the best performers through the credit crisis, is frequently held up as the acme of personalisation. As Gillian Tett, FT global markets editor, has observed: 'Employees [at Goldman] typically view themselves as being affiliated to the bank, not the business line, and there is a strong ethos of shared accountability.' But Goldman is the exception that proves the rule: the rest of the industry has relied heavily on bureaucratic approaches to risk management and the strategies of the major players have gradually converged over time.

How to personalise risk management

What does personalisation of risk management mean in practice? The concept has intuitive appeal, but many people struggle with how to balance the need for personalisation with broader systems of control and management. We suggest three necessary and supporting elements.

High-quality insight. Those who make decisions require good quality information, effective analytical tools and the competence to interpret this information. But it is rare for all these things to come together. It is more likely for decisions to be made with poor insight from self-interested sources, and with the relevant information fragmented across different parts of the company.

For example, one study has shown that mortgage loans securitised and sold on to non-banks in the early 2000s were far more likely to end up in default than when they were sold to affiliates of the originator. It is not surprising that banks that were selling loans had a different level of focus on the likelihood of default than those that held such loans to maturity. What is more surprising is that regulators and investors did not concern themselves more with this potential bias.

Effective personalisation of risk management is, therefore, about building a system that puts the right information into the hands of those making decisions, and then transforming that information into insight through experience.

Here is one example of how this works in a different setting. The UK police force gathers intelligence on a daily basis about criminal activities, community affairs and so on. Usually these are dealt with quickly and without note, but occasionally an incident escalates and becomes more serious. To better alert themselves to these escalations, the police have instituted a 'critical incident' approach, in which an employee of any rank can call together a cross-force group to pull together all the available information about an incident, and make a decision on how to react. Critical incidents only arise occasionally, but they provide an effective way of quickly bringing to bear the disparate views on an issue and reaching a thoughtful decision.

> **Most companies get personal accountability wrong**

Personal accountability. Effective risk management requires personal accountability, but most companies get this wrong as well. Sometimes there are too many decision makers, or the decision maker is too far removed from the action to feel any genuine responsibility. And often there is no link between the decisions taken and the rewards provided.

For example, in recent years, banks traded in risky securities to optimise short-term profits without giving due regard to the appropriate cost of capital or the long-term behaviour of these securities. Many people have argued that a large factor in the creation of the current financial crisis was this focus on short-term accounting profit and the reward systems aligned with it.

Instead, we need a system where personal accountability is rewarded, and where the individual or team with high-quality insight is also the one making the decision. For example, one of the basic principles that every airline captain knows is: make risk decisions at the appropriate level. Appropriate here means the level where the individual has the necessary experience and maturity to make a good decision. The captain may delegate specific decisions to engineering specialists or dispatchers, but the decision to fly the plane rests with him or her – not on the wishes of the air traffic controllers or the airline's chief executive.

This logic has clear applicability to the business world. Some of the best performers through the credit crisis, such as JPMorgan Chase and Goldman Sachs, were well known for their collegial, team-based decision processes, built on open debate, intellectual honesty, and sufficient self confidence to take contrarian decisions.

Supportive culture. The informal norms of behaviour in a company – its culture – should support the principles of high-quality insight and personal accountability. But all too often, these informal norms end up undermining the effectiveness of decision making. Some companies exhibit a fear culture where bad news is hidden from top executives; some are purely mercenary, where everyone looks out for themselves; some suffer from chronic risk aversion, with almost zero tolerance for false-positive errors.

Of course, there is no simple way to build a supportive culture. It takes many years of consistent messages and actions from leaders. But there are, nonetheless, a couple of basic principles that can be applied.

One is the need for transparency of purpose. Consider, for example, a leading mining company that committed a decade ago to eliminating one type of risk: employee injuries at work. All leaders signed up to this goal, all employees were trained on the company's safety standards, measures of lost-time injuries were monitored for all sites, and managers' compensation was linked to safety. Today, all meetings – even those in white collar environments – start with a safety update. Safety thinking is deeply ingrained in the minds of individuals throughout the company, and the safety record is impressive. Cultural transformation, in other words, is possible when it is tied to a very clear purpose that everyone can identify, and when it is reinforced through consistency of action. To return to the police force example earlier, a key feature of the 'critical incident' model is to acknowledge the efforts of the individual who calls it, even if it proves to be a false alarm.

The other principle is a refusal to simplify the big picture. Studies have been conducted of nuclear power plants and aircraft carriers where errors can have catastrophic consequences, and they have sought to understand how these 'high reliability' organisations function. It has emerged that one of the key features is that individual employees – involved, for example, in routine maintenance activities – are expected to take responsibility for seeing how their work fits into the big picture. So, rather than compartmentalising every task, employees are encouraged to look across and to understand how their work has implications for others.

This approach has obvious relevance in the financial services industry. As one leading hedge fund manager explained: 'We need to remain humble. I don't claim I know the answers; that is the golden rule. Strengths become weaknesses in a dislocation. We make our biggest mistakes where people claim we are strong.'

Conclusion

The credit crisis was brought about by the accumulation of a large number of circumstantial factors, but it was exacerbated and ultimately triggered by poor risk management decisions, and structures, at many large financial services companies. By turning the spotlight on these weaknesses, we have identified some key principles for effective risk management, not just in financial services but in other sectors as well.

But there is one important caveat. Good decision making in the world of financial services is not just about making objectively correct decisions, it is also about making decisions in the context of rapidly changing market conditions. Even the best decisions can look foolish in retrospect if market forces change fundamentally.

So, if the first challenge is how to make better quality decisions, the second challenge is learning how to adapt them to accommodate the market. But that is a matter for a separate article.

The challenges facing leadership

It is hard to dispute that we are living through the worst economic crisis since 1929 and that it is much more than just a trade cycle downturn. By **Rob Goffee** and **Gareth Jones**

The global financial system has changed fundamentally and we do not yet know what the new paradigm will look like. We do know, however, that leadership is more important than ever. Organisations that are well-led have a much better chance of surviving these turbulent times. This is not the occasion to take your eye off critical processes of leadership development – and smart organisations know this.

Perhaps the most significant contribution of good leadership is the provision of meaning and purpose. As the writer Studs Terkel famously observed: 'Work is about daily meaning as well as daily bread; for recognition as well as cash; in short, for a sort of life rather than a Monday through Friday sort of dying…. We have a right to ask of work that it include meaning, recognition, astonishment and life.'

Organisational attrition is in danger of crushing the very creative spirit that is essential to lifting us out of the current malaise. In the knowledge economy, which is critical to the future of western Europe, the challenge is not to follow tradition and attempt to 'get more' from your clever employees. Open any conventional management textbook on organisational behaviour and you will find an obsession with extracting more value from recalcitrant workers through the latest fashionable techniques of 'motivation', 'engagement', pursuit of 'discretionary effort' and so on.

“ Smart leadership is essential to retaining your valuable, clever people ” Our view is almost the opposite. The task is to make your organisation more attractive to your already valuable, clever people. While researching our new book, Clever – Leading Your Smartest, Most Creative People, we frequently observed talented individuals turned off by bureaucratic processes, internal politics and, above all, inadequate leadership.

Leading in a downturn

So what are the essential ingredients of successful leadership in these troubled times?

The conventional wisdom has it that in uncertain times the role of the leader is to provide certainty, to be a rock against which the waves of disruption will crash. But our observations suggest that the most effective among them offer not the illusion of certainty, but the promise of constant change and adaptability. If we have learnt anything – not just from the current economic difficulties but from the economic history of the 20th century – it is that no sector is immune to the threat of disruptive change. Capitalism remains an aggressive and acquisitive social system. As Karl Marx put it, 'one capitalist kills many'.

Leaders cannot see the future, but they can and must communicate a compelling picture of what the future might look like. It has become an overused concept, but vision remains important. The leader must communicate what the organisation stands for, what its purpose is and which values give it coherence. It is when organisations are in difficulties that their true commitment to core values are most severely tested. In addition, in a world awash with information overload, the leader's voice must be distinctive in order to excite others to exceptional performance.

Barack Obama, US president, exhibits just that quality of exceptional communication skills that has convinced the US electorate that despite the turmoil, change is possible.

As companies contract and inevitably become more political, there is a lesson for business leaders. On the one hand, they must understand the political manoeuvring and on the other they must remain – and be seen to remain – above it.

One preliminary conclusion arising from these observations is that in turbulent times steadfastness is a leadership virtue. Not in the sense of having a fixed view of what will happen next, but by being true to a set of core values. A naïve reading of this point would suggest that all the leader has to do is be their authentic self. But that is not enough. Change will require that leaders play different roles in different contexts. In our previous book, Why Should Anyone Be Led By You?, we noted that effective leadership involves a complex balancing act between using your authentic differences and adapting your behaviours to context. Being authentic is not about being the same all the time. The most effective leaders are authentic chameleons. The chameleon always adapts to context but remains a chameleon.

❝ In turbulent times, leaders need to be true to a set of care values ❞

Effective leadership requires managing a series of inspirational tensions that are especially significant in a downturn.

First, since leadership is always contextual – leading in a pharmaceutical company is different from leading in a shipyard – so the ability to adapt is vital. Effective leaders have a real sense of what is going on in their company. The old fad of 'managing by walking around' contained one great truth: you need to be in a position to collect soft data, to know what is happening on the shop floor before the management information system tells you.

Business leaders will also be tested by their capacity to articulate meaning and make sense of a difficult situation. Rudolph Giuliani, mayor of New York at the time of the terrorist attacks of 2001, was not only in the right place at the right time, he also offered New Yorkers hope for the future. As the tragedy unfolded, he assured them that New York would be back.

In much the same way, Andrew Higginson, finance director of UK retailer Tesco, recently signalled that the current unpopularity of the retail banks represented a significant opportunity for them to further apply their popular brand to the financial services business.

Michael O'Leary, chief executive of low-cost airline Ryanair, goes even further. He welcomes the recession. In his view, it will kill off poor operators and show what a great business Ryanair is.

Each of these examples demonstrates that effective leaders both read context and rewrite it. In difficult times, the danger is that business leaders are trapped by circumstance and become entirely reactive. Skilled leadership involves not just reacting but proactively and constructively reshaping events.

Second, a strong focus may be a prerequisite for survival. Leaders will be energetically focused on hard-nosed, tough prioritisation, including cutbacks and cost control. These actions are likely to be painful. They are the familiar accompaniment to recession. But they should not come at the expense of team or organisational cohesion. If people must leave, they must leave with dignity. Recessions are not an excuse to be nasty. Nor are they a time to throw away the cultural characteristics that hold organisations together and make some of them special.

Finally, sensing situations and building team cohesion will require social closeness to ensure a company-wide sense that 'we are all in this together'. The criticism targeted at some senior business leaders, for example, stems from the fact that they continue to pay themselves bonuses while others suffer.

But strong 'identification with the troops' should not limit the ability of leaders to step back and see the bigger picture. Indeed, paradoxically, this is a key situation sensing skill. Leaders will need to make tough decisions and social closeness cannot get in the way.

There is no recipe for good leadership but, as we have argued, it does involve several tensions. Do not claim to know the future but articulate a vision. Understand the politics but remain above them. Respond quickly to situational demands but act to reshape them. Focus relentlessly on task but build team cohesion. Identify with your employees but be prepared to take a step back. And be your authentic self but recognise that you have different, and difficult, roles to play.

About the authors

Paul A. Argenti is professor of corporate communication at Tuck School of Business, Dartmouth College.

Julian Birkinshaw is professor of strategic management at London Business School.

Arturo Bris is professor of finance at IMD, a research fellow at the Yale International Center for Finance, and a research associate at the European Corporate Governance Institute.

Murillo Campello is the I. B. E. distinguished professor of finance at the University of Illinois at Urbana-Champaign.

Laurence Capron is professor of strategy at Insead and research director of the Insead-Wharton alliance.

Robert Clemen is professor and faculty director of the Corporate Sustainability Initiative at the Fuqua School of Business, Duke University.

Vasant Dhar is professor of information systems, group head, IOMS-Information Systems and co-director, Center for Digital Economy Research, NYU Stern School of Business.

B. Espen Eckbo is Tuck Centennial professor of finance and founding director of the Center for Corporate Governance at Tuck School of Business, Dartmouth College.

Nuno Fernandes is professor of finance at IMD and a Lamfalussy research fellow of the European Central Bank.

Pankaj Ghemawat is Anselmo Rubiralta professor of global strategy at Iese Business School and the author of 'Redefining Global Strategy: Crossing Borders in a World Where Differences Still Matter'.

Michael Gibbs is clinical professor of economics and human resources at the University of Chicago Booth School of Business. He is also co-author, with Edward Lazear, of 'Personnel Economics in Practice'.

Rob Goffee is professor of organisational behaviour and director of the Innovation Exchange at London Business School.

John Graham is the D. Richard Mead Jr. Family professor of finance at the Fuqua School of Business, Duke University.

Lynda Gratton is professor of management practice at London Business School and founder of the Hot Spots Research Institute (**www.hotspotsmovement.com**). She is the author of 'Glow: How You Can Radiate Energy, Innovation and Success'.

Ranjay Gulati is the Jaime and Josefina Chua Tiampo professor of business administration at Harvard Business School and the author of 'From Inside-Out to Outside-In: Reconfiguring Organisational Silos to Build Customer Centric Organisations'.

Neal A. Hartman is a senior lecturer in behavioural and policy sciences at Sloan School of Management, MIT.

Campbell Harvey is the J. Paul Sticht professor of international business at the Fuqua School of Business, Duke University.

Thomas M. Hout is visiting professor at the University of Hong Kong's School of Business and fellow of the Center for Emerging Market Enterprise at the Fletcher School of Law and Diplomacy.

Michael G. Jacobides is associate professor of strategic and international management at London Business School and the Sumantra Gloshal Fellow at the Advanced Institute of Management.

Huw Jenkins is executive in residence at London Business School.

Katherine E. Jocz is a research associate at Harvard Business School and co-author, with John A. Quelch, of 'Greater Good: How Good Marketing Makes for Better Democracy'.

Gareth Jones is fellow of the Centre for Management Development at London Business School and visiting professor at IE Business School in Madrid.

Kevin Kaiser is affiliate professor of finance and director of the International Executive programme at Insead.

Jean-Pierre Lehmann is professor of international economy at IMD, founding director of The Evian Group and co-author, with John Haffner and Tomas Casas I Klett, of 'Japan's Open Future: An Agenda for Global Citizenship'.

Peter Lorange is the Kristian Gerhard Jebsen professor of international shipping and former president of IMD.

Ilian Mihov is professor of economics at Insead and Novartis chaired professor of management and environment.

Nitin Nohria is Richard P. Chapman professor of business adminstration, senior associate dean and director of faculty development at Harvard Business School.

John A. Quelch is Lincoln Filene professor of business administration at Harvard Business School and a visiting professor at Ceibs.

Suzanne Rosselet-McCauley is the deputy director of the World Competitiveness Center at IMD.

Andrew Scott is professor and joint chair of economics at London Business School.

Christian Seelos is adjunct professor of strategic management at Iese Business School.

ManMohan S. Sodhi is professor in operations management at Cass Business School.

Stefan Stern is the FT's management writer.

Paul Strebel is the Sandoz Family Foundation professor and director of the High Performance Boards programme at IMD.

Donald Sull is professor of management practice in strategic and international management and faculty director of executive education at London Business School.

Arun Sundararajan is associate professor of information, operations and management sciences and NEC Faculty Fellow, NYU Stern School of Business.

Jayashankar M. Swaminathan is Kay and Van Weatherspoon distinguished professor of operations, technology and innovation management at the University of North Carolina's Kenan-Flagler Business School, and the author of 'Indian Economic Superpower: Fiction or Future?'.

Christopher S. Tang is professor in operations management at the UCLA Anderson School of Management where he holds the Edward W. Carter chair in business administration.

Daniel Vermeer is executive director at the Corporate Sustainability Initiative at the Fuqua School of Business, Duke University.

Russell Walker is assistant director of the Zell Center for Risk Research at the Kellogg School of Management.

Batia Mishan Wiesenfeld is professor of management at NYU Stern School of Business, Robert and Dale Atkins Rosen Faculty Fellow and Daniel P. Paduano Faculty Fellow.

Index